Architecture and Democracy

by Deyan Sudjic
with Helen Jones

Architecture and Democracy

by Deyan Sudjic
with Helen Jones

Laurence King

Published in 2001 by
Laurence King Publishing
in association with Glasgow City Council
Laurence King Publishing is an
imprint of Calmann & King Ltd
71 Great Russell Street
London WC1B 3BP
Telephone +44 20 7430 8850
Fax +44 20 7430 8880
e-mail enquiries@calmann-king.co.uk
www.laurence-king.com

Distributed in the United States and Canada
by te Neues Publishing Company
16 West 22nd Street, New York, NY 10010
Tel: 212-627 9090
Fax: 212-627 9511
www.teneus.com

A catalogue record for this book
is available from the British Library.

UK ISBN 1 85669 267 1
US ISBN 3-8238-5565-4

Designed by Wordsearch

Printed in China

Architecture and Democracy
is dedicated to Enric Miralles, architect
of the Scottish Parliament and Clive
Wainwright, expert on Pugin, without whom
the exhibition and this book would never
have happened.

Exhibition curators
Deyan Sudjic and Helen Jones

Exhibition Design
Peter Murray and Samantha Worthington
Wordsearch

Exhibition Graphics
Sheran Forbes
Wordsearch

Book Graphics
Sandra Grubic
Wordsearch

Research
Libby Sellers
Restructure Ltd

Audio-visual
55°

Contents

Foreword
by The Rt. Honourable Sir David Steel KBE MSP

At a time of great political change in the United Kingdom occasioned by the movement of devolved powers to Scotland and Wales, it gives me great pleasure to recommend a book on parliamentary buildings and the debating chambers within them.

"Architecture and Democracy" outlines the development of structures (both open air and enclosed) from the time of classical Greece and Rome to the construction of the Scottish Parliament and the Welsh Assembly.

The respect that we pay to these buildings and the work that goes on within them to make society a better and safer place for us all is a key indicator of progress or its lack.

Of particular interest to myself are those chapters describing the Scottish Parliament. Following the deaths of both Donald Dewar and Enric Miralles, the two most significant figures so far as the actual design and construction of the buildings themselves are concerned, it is vital for the democratic process in Scotland that the work they began so well is brought to a successful conclusion. This book will I believe contribute to the process of understanding the progressive development of Scottish democracy, so necessary for the garnering of support both within and without Scotland.

Presiding Officer of the Scottish Parliament

Architecture and Democracy an exploration of the design of

For at least 2,500 years people have assembled to participate in and observe democracy in action. The environments in which democratic debate takes place can be seen as a physical expression of mankind's relationship with the ideals of democracy. The democratic imperative – defined as the citizens possessing the right to be involved with the political decisions which affect their daily lives – has created some of the world's most highly charged, resonant and accomplished works of architecture. Parliament buildings act as a continuing reminder of the aspirations of nations and their values.

This book, which grew out of an exhibition originally staged as part of Glasgow's year as UK City of Architecture and Design 1999, considers the relationship between parliaments and their architectural expression. The outer structures and inner spaces of those forums have been created since ancient times to embody the voice of democracy and to provide a platform for it. They attempt to represent the values of democracy and of nationhood.

In form they range from the amphitheatres of classical civilisations to the outdoor Viking assemblies, the annual Icelandic *Althingi* and the Isle of Man Tynwald. Symbolically successful parliament buildings capture the spirit of the people they exist to serve, epitomised by Charles Barry and A W N Pugin's Gothic Palace of Westminster and the monumental dome of the US Capitol. Architectural vision at the service of democratic ideals has created a diverse range of structures, from the bold utopian visions at Chandigarh and Brasilia and Dacca, to the recent reconstitution of historic buildings such as the Reichstag.

Remarkably, at the beginning of the twenty first century three significant contributions to the architecture of democracy are presently under construction in the UK. On 26 January 1998 Donald Dewar announced a competition to select an architect-led design team for the new Scottish Parliament. Winners Enric Miralles and RMJM designed a complex of buildings to house the Scottish Parliament. Their designs are presently taking shape on site in Edinburgh and will be an internationally recognisable representation of Scotland and the resumption of its parliament after 300 years.

In October 1998 Lord Callaghan and his design team recommended the Richard Rogers Partnership to design the Welsh National Assembly building. Lord Rogers' vision of a transparent and public assembly building at the site of Cardiff Bay is due to open in 2003. And in London Lord Foster, the British architect of the new Reichstag, is creating the riverside Greater London Authority building as home for the Mayor of London.

To varying degrees the processes of governments are influenced by the buildings in which they are accommodated, and in turn parliament buildings reflect the political ideologies of governments. Within the bricks and mortar or concrete and steel of parliament buildings politicians talk to each other, agree and disagree with each other, occasionally come to blows with each other, make and break rules, and determine the framework for society through which the future is defined. Design provides something akin to a stage set for the theatre of political debate.

Winston Churchill opened the debate on the rebuilding of the House of Commons in October 1943, with the ringing declaration after severe bomb damage, "We shape our buildings and afterwards our buildings shape us." Churchill succeeded in his wish to rebuild the bombed chamber in its original form, "The whole character of the British parliamentary institution depends upon the fact that the House of Commons is an oblong and not a semi-circular structure."

The chamber, as the place where a legislative assembly meets, plays a central role in the democratic decision making process. While Britain and many of its former colonies have adopted the confrontational chamber of facing sets of benches – the result of a historical accident showing the origins of the British Parliament in the choir stalls of the former chapel of the Palace of Westminster – in Western democracy the favoured arrangement is the semi-circle. The amphitheatre model, derived from classical precedents, ensures that all those present can hear and see the person speaking at all times. Seating arrangements in semi-circular chambers vary according to national preference, the normal arrangement being for political parties to sit as groups in semi-circular chambers. For example, in Germany all those present are allocated a specific seat, in Ireland members sit according to party block, and European parliamentarians sit in party blocks. Russia and other Eastern states preferred an alternative form, the Duma being laid out in a class-room like arrangement where the cabinet is seated behind the podium facing the elected representatives.

The architectural envelopes that enclose parliaments reflect national tradition and democratic aspiration. Parliament buildings reflect the way countries see themselves, or more accurately, they are the three-dimensional realisation of how countries would like themselves to be seen. New Parliaments are constructed to house new governments in new nation states, to replace buildings damaged by fire or bombs, old Parliaments are refurbished to mark reunification, extensions are added to accommodate increasingly full-time parliamentarians.

While the twentieth century saw the construction of more brand new parliaments than any other preceding period, parliaments are rarely fixed institutions. More often they are accommodated in buildings that are modified at regular intervals throughout their history showing political evolution and shifting national history. Scenes of order and disorder, drama and inertia, within these buildings reflect the political state of any country. The storming of the Reichstag on May Day 1945 was deemed so important it was re-enacted for Soviet cameras days later. And it remains a defining moment.

Footage of President Nikita Kruschev losing his temper to the extent of removing his shoe and banging it on his desk at the United Nations Assembly, New York, 12 October 1960, no longer exists. The camera did record the occasion in 1998 when Vladimir Zhirinivsky threw water at rivals when he was not allowed to speak in the Russian parliament, and brawling female MPs in the Taiwanese parliament. The ceiling of the Cortes, Madrid still bears the scars of bullets from the machine pistols of mutinous members of the Guardia Civil on 23 February 1981, President Jayewardene broadcast to Sri Lanka splattered with blood from a hand grenade explosion detonated inside the new Parliament, 18 August 1987 and the Italian parliament boasts hours of footage of fighting representatives. In contrast both chambers at the Palace of Westminster frequently show rows of empty benches indicative of the removal of political decision making from the House of Commons and Lords. As Tony Benn commented "we have been watching the decline in the process of parliament". Ironically, as these powers decline the quantity of television coverage of parliament increases. This also suggests that the confrontational layout of opposed benches can foster gentler politics than amphitheatres.

Soviet troops storm the Reichstag
Berlin, 30 April 1945

Nikita Kruschev's anti-imperialist outburst
United Nations Assembly, New York, 12 October 1960

President of the United States, John F. Kennedy addressing the Dáil
June 1963

Guardia Civil enter Spain's Parliament and terrorise MPs with firearms
Cortes, Madrid, 23 February 1981

Heated exchanges and scuffles between Italian MPs before voting for a new State President
Italian Parliament, Rome, 13 May 1992

Representative Su Chih-Yang accuses two male Nationalist party members of being peeping toms and brawl ensues
National Assembly, Taiwan, 3 June 1994

Boris Yeltsin persuades mutinous troops not to destroy Russia's new democracy
Duma, Moscow, 1 March 1996

Democratic precedents

Chapter one

Democratic precedents

Ever since antiquity the classical ideal of a universal civilisation based on broadly democratic principles has dominated the practice of politics in the Western world. Classical democracy not only influenced the formation of later constitutions, it also created an architectural legacy which has dominated both the form and style of parliament buildings to the present day. An alternative precedent originated in the middle of the first century in Iceland. From the outdoor Viking assemblies a distinctive Scandinavian political tradition developed which may be considered as a root of a more specifically national approach to parliamentary architecture.

The practical and symbolic precedent for democratic society began in Athens 2,500 years ago, democracy, derived from *demokratia* (*demos* – the people, or the citizenry, and *kratos* – rule), being a form of government in which the people rule themselves, either directly, as in the small city-states of ancient Greece, or through representatives, such as the elected members of Westminster.

The Ancient Greeks created an organised civilisation based upon the political ideal of equality among its citizens, liberty and respect for the law and justice. These beliefs have shaped political thinking in the West and the modern liberal notion that human beings are "individuals" with "rights" stems directly from the principles of classical Greek democracy. During the eighth century BC the formula for urban living arrived with the emergence of the *polis* or city-state within the world of ancient Greece. Almost all our political vocabulary from "political" on, is rooted in the ancient Greek city-state which worked as a designated politically independent community within a specified territory, usually with aspirations for the colonisation of neighbouring states.

Participation in the activities of the *polis* was a central part of the definition of Greek citizenship. Qualification for citizenship was rigorous; in Athens the *demos* consisted entirely of adult males of strictly Athenian descent. This system of qualification for citizenship excluded all women, slaves and resident aliens and was further restricted by Pericles to those who were the sons of an Athenian father, himself a citizen, and an Athenian mother.

The Greeks were the first people to create societies based on the concept of citizenship. A citizen was someone who in Aristotle's view participated in "giving judgement and holding office". Citizenship meant direct participation in public affairs, including in legislative and judicial functions, a system which in sharp contrast to practically every previous alternative allowed for the direct participation of each citizen. Belief in *isonomia* – equality of respect and treatment under the law – enabled the citizens of Athens to overthrow and resist tyranny, or one-man dictatorship, and to place political power "into the centre", as the Greeks put it. That is, to transfer power from the closed world of the royal palace to the open spaces of the Agora. Decisions previously taken in secret were replaced by public debate. Political power became the property, not of one man, but of all citizens.

In *The Peloponnesian War* Thucydides recalls the famous funeral speech attributed to Pericles. The passage provides insight into how the world's first democracy worked and what it meant in practical terms to the Athenian citizens.

"Our constitution is called a democracy because power is in the hands not of a minority but of the whole people. Here each individual is interested not only in his own affairs but in the affairs of the state as well: even those who are mostly occupied with their own business are extremely well-informed on general politics – this is a peculiarity of ours: we do not say that a man who takes no interest in politics is a man who minds his own business;

Pynx, Athens
One of the earliest meeting places for political assembly was the hillside of the Pnyx, west of the Acropolis in Greece.

we say that he has no business here at all."

Periclean Athens may not have regarded women, slaves or foreigners as worthy of civic rights, but those privileged enough to qualify for citizenship enjoyed the first flowering of a democratic system of government in the city state. Citizens were equal before the law and enjoyed an equal opportunity to speak in the city's political assembly. Important decisions were debated in a public forum and voted on by the citizenry as a whole. In the fourth century BC the power and scale of the *demos* meant that politics were carried out in the open. Athenians gathered on the semi-circular hillside of the Pnyx to the west of the Acropolis. The logical approach to the organisation of the polis made it inconceivable that a site would have been chosen so unsuitable for the purposes of

a popular assembly as to need the addition of a costly artificial auditorium. In the fifth century the Pnyx was defined by semi-circular masonry which formed the base of a retaining wall that rose to a considerable height, supporting a theatre-like structure capable of seating several thousand people. Projecting from the upper platform at the centre of the chord of the semi-circular area stood a cube of rock, eleven feet square and five feet high, approached on either side by a flight of steps leading to the top; this block, which Curtius supposes to have been the primitive altar of Zeus, may be identified with the orators' bema. Its shape ensured that every participant could not see just the speaker, but all those present.

Greek city-states allowed all citizens to assemble together at regular intervals for legislative and other purposes. The *demos*

Pynx, Athens
Provided a fitting location for Athenian political assembly which responded to the natural landscape of the hillside site

held sovereign power, that is, supreme authority, to engage in legislative and judicial functions. This sovereign assembly of the people was known in Athens as the Ekklesia, at Sparta as the Apella and in Rome variously as the Comitia Centuriata or the Concilium Plebis. In large cities, such as Athens, thousands of people attended such meetings. Those citizens present were assigned a seat, thought to be allocated according to their tribal allegiance. The ideal of the popular democratic assembly was thus established. However, Athenian democracy was a highly exclusive form of government. There is little trace of representative government in the modern sense in Athenian history, though certain of the magistrates had a quasi-representative character. The Pnyx, preceded by a sacrifice to Zeus, was valued as the seat of an ancient cult and meetings of the Ekklesia had a religious character.

Meetings of the Ekklesia took place every nine days and required a minimum of 6,000 citizens. The Athenian police patrolled the streets shepherding citizens from the north end of the Agora to the assembly, using a length of rope covered in red powder. Any citizen with red marks found outside the assembly was punished. At the assembly people spoke for themselves, rather than relying on representatives to resolve communal decisions that faced them. In the main officers were elected from the most powerful, usually the wealthiest families. Speakers were predominantly aristocrats who had studied the art of speaking. The best orator was considered to be the best citizen.

The model of direct democracy for a selected stratum of the population is problematic except in small states. In larger states representatives become necessary.

Cicero and Catilina in the Roman Senate
This modern fresco in the Italian Senate depicting the events of 50BC serves to remind contemporary politicians of classical precedents

Direct democracy has not been without its problems. Aristotle drew a distinction between what he called polity or constitutional government, meaning the rule of the majority of the free and equal citizens, and monarchy and aristocracy, the rule respectively of an individual and of a minority consisting of the best citizens. Aristotle's view of direct democracy as ochlocracy, or mob-rule, was rooted in his experience of the Athenian democracy that had by his day degenerated far below the ideals of the fifth century BC, when it reached its zenith under Pericles. War in Aristotle's day was endemic and politics were often violent and sometimes corrupt.

Cities were typically controlled by kingships at this time but later became dominated by clan and tribal hierarchies. City-states adapted constitutions which followed a pattern widespread throughout Greek civilisation. With the growth of empire and nation states in the classical world this narrow parochial type of democracy became unmanageable. A rigid distinction between citizens and non-citizens became progressively more difficult to maintain. Communities of a few thousand people living in close proximity to each other meant the population became too large and the distance too great for regular assemblies of all qualified citizens. This problem has been solved in various ways in different countries at different historical periods. Some have adopted a property qualification, while full democracy was based on the extension of citizenship to all adult persons with or without distinction of sex. The essence of modern representative government is that the people do not govern themselves, but periodically elect those who govern on their behalf. The city-states of classical Greece lost their dominant position after the death of Alexander the Great and the next experiment in the organisation of society took place in Rome, an experiment whose impact spread across the Roman Empire. The political historian Kenneth Minogue noted, "We inherit our ideas from the Greeks, but our practices from the Romans ... All Europeans, however, have benefited from the inheritance of two quite distinct vocabularies with which to explore political life: the political vocabulary of the Greeks – police, politics itself – and the civic vocabulary of the Romans – civility, citizen, civilisation. Both the architecture and the terminology of American politics, for example, are notably Roman."

Like the Greeks the Romans held an assembly of adult males based on a hierarchical system. The oldest and most permanent element in the Roman constitution was the senate or Council of Elders. Originally members were the heads of leading families who in general formed the upper council of the governmental system.

The legendary origin of the ancient Roman senate goes back to Romulus, who selected 100 of his subjects to form an advisory body. By 509 BC the council already contained 300 members. Throughout the monarchical period senators were appointed under the direction of the king and consisted entirely of patricians. Senators retained their position only for as long as they retained the favour of the reigning monarch. A king could change his advisers during his reign, and a new king could certainly refrain from summoning all those senators convened by his predecessors. The first plebeian senator mentioned by Livy is P. Licinius Calvus and there is no evidence of a plebeian senator before the year 401 BC. Senators were identifiable in public life by their dress, the senatorial insignia defined by the broad stripe (*latus clavus*) on the tunic and the red shoe (*calceus mulleus*) was worn by both senators and their sons during some periods of the Roman Empire.

The Senatorial Assembly met regularly to discuss the political affairs of the day in the Curia or Senate House. Located to the west of the Forum Romanum, it is believed the original Senate House was built by the Etruscan king Tullus Hostilius. His Senate House was rebuilt several times on the same site. In 80 BC it was replaced by the Curia Julia. Within forty years the Curia Julia was destroyed by fire. Julius Caesar rebuilt it in 44 BC and the task was completed by Augustus. The Curia was restored by Domitian and rebuilt by Diocletian and others to the original design, following a fire in 283. Today, that building survives as the church of Sant' Adriano.

At 21 metres high the building of fired brick faced in concrete and marble with an upper layer of decorated stucco had a significant presence in the city. Senators assembled on rows of wooden seats on steps. The most senior sat on the front benches nearest to the orator. By the time of Augustus the senate had nearly 1,000 members, so many in fact that if all senators attended there were too many to be seated.

Hierarchy again resolved the situation, forcing the youngest, least important senators to stand on the top step at the back. During meetings of the senate the doors were left open so the next generation of senators could observe the business of the house.

The powers of the senate were extensive. It dealt with the control of foreign policy in that took charge of external relations of the cities which were scattered throughout the provinces of the Roman Empire. The senate had the power to sanction acts of state and exercised a police control in Rome in sudden emergencies. Traditionally the senate held the power to act as the king's executive representative when he was absent and to assist him in law making. The abolition of the monarchical system and its replacement by two annually elected consuls did not at first bring any important change to the position of the senate. In the early days of the Roman Republic the senate remained primarily an advisory body. As a consultative body, meeting only at their pleasure, the consuls were subordinate to the chief magistrates of the senate. By the last two centuries of the Republic a great change had taken place and the senate had become an independent, automatically constituted body,

Rome developed from a single city into an empire, that looked back to its roots for architectural language.

Even today senate is the term used to define the upper legislative house in various bicameral parliaments and Rome's senate is regarded as the early precipitator of the great representative of republican

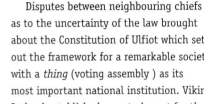

Þingvollr, Assembly Plains, Iceland
Iceland's Viking settlers established one of the world's earliest democratic societies, the *Althingi*, which met annually in the open air at *Þingvollr* until 1799

institutions. The role of the senate as a designated second chamber of the legislature remains in place in France, Italy, the United States and other nations and is represented in British legislature by the House of Lords. In Scottish law, the Lords of Session – that is judges – are called Senators of the College of Justice, which is itself referred to as a senate.

The architectural legacy of the Greek and Roman civilisations, the temples of the Greek world and the religious, civil and military architecture of Rome, has provided the grammar of architectural language for most of the civilised world throughout the five centuries between the Renaissance and our own time.

Because of the dominance of the classical, alternative architectural precedents for democratic institutions are not as well known. If Athens is one root for the world's democratic traditions, Scandinavia offers another distinctive path.

Iceland's Viking settlers established one of the Western world's earliest democratic societies based on an assembly, the *Althingi*, that met annually from around 930 AD.

Disputes between neighbouring chiefs as to the uncertainty of the law brought about the Constitution of Ulfiot which set out the framework for a remarkable society, with a *thing* (voting assembly) as its most important national institution. Viking Iceland established a central moot for the whole island where a speaker adhered to a single set of laws. The *Althingi* met every summer at *Þingvollr* (Assembly Plains) on the Oxara (Axe River) in the south west of Iceland. The heart of the open-air assembly was a small grassy hill. At its centre the presiding official, the Law Speaker, took his seat. Most of those attending simply pitched tents for its two week duration. Leading figures, however, needed to establish a more elaborate base to reflect their status. These took the form of turf booths with homespun cloth roofs. Some of these structures were quite large and were maintained on the same site for year after year. Participation in the main social event of the year was not limited to those directly involved in politics, disputes and legal cases. *Nial's Saga* records that brewers, craftsmen and merchants also contributed to the festival atmosphere, staying in their own booths while the *Althingi* was in session.

The Viking's *thing* or voting assembly of freemen became a widely adopted model for the governing institutions of many Germanic peoples. Although there were such assemblies throughout Scandinavia, the Icelandic *Althingi* was unusual in that it united an entire country under a single legal system, and without a monarch. When Norse Vikings settled in the Isle of Man they brought with them the concept of an open-air assembly of freemen. The earliest local records describe the Tynwald of 1228, when a battle resulted in the death of the Manx king Reginald. The Isle of Man Tynwald had many features similar to those of the open-air Icelandic *Althingi*: a Law Hill, enclosed and surrounded by a green; joined by a pathway on the east to a Court House; and a place of worship, St John's Church. The twelve foot high Tynwald Hill, an artificial mound covered in turf, is believed to contain earth from all the seventeen ancient parishes. For more than two centuries a protective canopy has been raised over the topmost of four circular platforms during the annual assembly.

The obscure origin of the British parliament may be traced to precedents such as the *Althingi* and more directly to the Anglo-Saxon Witanagemot, the assembly of wise men. When the Anglo-Saxons conquered Britain they brought with them their own laws and customs. Anglo-Saxon society was based around the central democratic organism, known as the Witanagemot. Members of the witan were primarily councillors whose actions informed the foundation of the popular parliament of England. The number of counsellors attending the meeting of the witan varied considerably from time to time. By the seventh and eighth centuries the larger kingdoms of Kent, Wessex, Mercia and Northumbria each had their own separate witan or council. As the number of kings decreased so too did the number of witans until early in the 9th century there was one king and one witan in all England. During the reign of King Edgar, the Witenagemot became the official legislative assembly, or parliament, of the extended estate with the king as its the chief power.

It consisted, in addition to the king, his sons and other relatives, of the bishops and later some abbots, of some under-kings and the aldermen of the shires or provinces, and a number of ministri or members of the royal household. A high proportion of members were routinely nominated by the king, so much so that eventually their number gradually increased until they outstripped that of all other members:

"In a Witenagemot held at Luton in November AD 931 were the two archbishops, two Welsh princes, seventeen bishops, fifteen ealdormen, five abbots and fifty-nine ministri. In another, that of Winchester of AD 934, were present the two archbishops, four Welsh kings, seventeen bishops, four abbots, twelve ealdormen and fifteen ministri ..."

Despite the fact that in theory witans had the power to elect a new king, the power of the witan varied according to the personality of the reigning king, being considerable under a weak ruler, but much less so under a strong one. With his councillors' consent the king promulgated laws, made grants of land, appointed bishops and aldermen, and discharged the other duties of government.

Throughout its history the Witenagemot appears to have had no fixed place of meeting. The assembly of members took place wherever the king and his court might be. In the later years of its existence, the assembly met at least three times a year, typically at Easter, Whitsuntide and Christmas. Almost immediately after the Norman Conquest the word fell into disuse. Despite the change in terminology, the memory of these prototypical democratic assemblies remains, visible in the indirect democratic legacy of both classical and Viking democratic precedents.

Classicism reborn

Classicism reborn

The political institutions established by the Athenian city-state and adopted and modified by the Republic of Rome have had an enduring impact on modern Western political practice and thought. The Greek political legacy is still reflected in the abundance of government buildings which act as a physical reminder of the classical origins of parliamentary democracy.

The classical language of architecture has been used more than any other to create monumental parliamentary buildings that both inspire and can also intimidate in their representation of the democratic ideal. As a showcase for political intention and the

pre-eminent symbol of the state parliament buildings embody national identity and historical consciousness. Politicians and architects have used an architecture drawing on past associations to assert the status of existing and developing democracies.

The rise of neo-classical architecture during the eighteenth century saw the establishment of the first purpose-built semi-circular chamber in Western democracy, housed in the Palladian Irish parliament building. Ever since, neo-classical architecture has dominated both the form and style of parliament buildings, the layout of parliament buildings

characterised by the great ceremonial spaces of the chamber, central hall and monumental entrance enclosed in a classical structure. Semi-circular debating chambers, tracing their roots to the bowl shaped assembly at the Pnyx of Athens and the amphitheatres of Rome, have provided a physical structure for democratic debate in countries as culturally diverse as America, France, Finland, Germany and India.

Ancient Greece and Rome were both predominantly oral cultures, based on popular participation in the affairs of the state with little centralised bureaucratic control. Classical practice was suppressed,

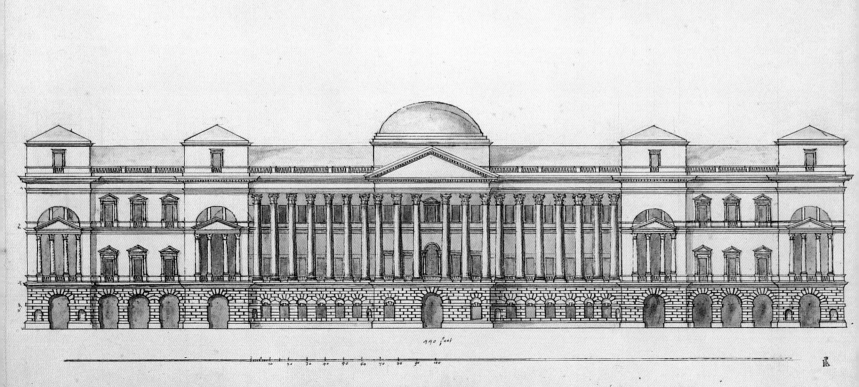

but not extinguished by the Dark Ages from which it re-emerged, only slightly modified by subsequent religious influences. Christian institutions required occasional debating forums for church government and the election of bishops. The overriding tendency was for the clergy to distance themselves from secular debate and maintain an interest only in divine governance using their influence where felt necessary on those who held power whether democratically obtained or not.

In the Western world the classical democratic model was gradually revived to house the representatives of larger populations first for the bourgeois parliaments of the eighteenth century such as Dublin and Washington and later for parliamentary systems based on universal suffrage. The architectural language of their Parliaments relied upon an established political tradition to reflect its authority. None more so than the fledgling United States of America which looked back to Greece and Rome to legitimise its own republic.

The predominant influence on British architectural ideas encapsulating democratic expression was classical. Despite the fact that the most famous parliamentary building, the "mother of parliaments", is Gothic in its detail, it relies upon Grecian symmetry in its plan.

Most British governments who wished to imply democratic consent for the imperial idea built classical parliamentary buildings throughout their empire. Sir Herbert Baker's buildings at Pretoria and New Delhi for example are emphatically classicist in their derivation.

The idea that classical architecture could embody the democratic ideal continued well into the twentieth century. It was both a self-conscious claim on Athenian democracy as a legitimisation for much younger states, and also an appeal to a cosmopolitan tradition, beyond any single national identity. The internationalism of the modern movement became a twentieth-century embodiment of the same pan-national tendency. For example, the United Nations building, in New York, completed in 1952, was intended to symbolise the rational ideals of the member states. Aesthetically, it attempted to supplant national traditions and prejudices with a universal, progressive design able to communicate the aspirations of the new world organization.

The question of an appropriate national architectural style has exercised Britain ever since the Act of Union in 1707. The Gothic style specified for the rebuilt Palace of Westminster was intended to be and has become central to the identity of the British people. The symbolic presence of the buildings at Westminster, most notably the iconic clock tower, have become so central to the national consciousness of the United Kingdom that it seems inconceivable that the buildings could have been entirely different, classical even.

Throughout the eighteenth century, designs for a British Senate House and for the Parliament House of imperial London played a large part in the ambitions and rivalries of British architects who dreamed of the chance of a commission on a grand scale that would live up to classical precedents. Proposals for a neo-classical Houses of Parliament were presented by most of the leading architects of the day including James Adam, William Kent and Sir John Soane.

From 1733 to 1739 William Kent worked on designs for a new Houses of Parliament, a great rectangular building designed to stand immediately to the south of Westminster Hall. The design combined elements from ancient Rome, Palladio and Inigo Jones; its architectural expression was characteristic of the style developed by Lord Burlington and Kent. The plan demonstrated a shrewd understanding of the practical and ceremonial functions of the Georgian parliament and Kent proposed various shaped plans for the House of Commons chamber, including circular, elliptical and some with the oppositional arrangement that existed in St Stephen's chapel, but there is no indication that the drawings were officially approved.

Between 1760 and 1762, the young James Adam designed a new Parliament as a theoretical exercise while studying in Rome under Charles Louis Clérisseau, the neo-classical architect who had been Robert Adam's friend and artistic mentor in Rome. The Scottish born Adam's unfulfilled monumental scheme included a design for a capital, a new British order, including the lion and unicorn, and is thought to have included the design for a Scottish order, which uses thistles as a symbol of national identity.

Sir John Soane, the master of inventive modern classical architecture, designed both a British Senate House and a Parliament. The greatest artistic disappointment of Soane's long career was the shelving of his design of 1794 for extensive additions to the old Houses of Parliament, which almost amounted to complete rebuilding. In the Royal Staircase, anteroom and gallery of 1823 Soane was able to create something of his design. His Scala Reggia was a casualty of the fire of 1834 and was subsequently demolished as classicism gave way to Gothic in the architectural "battle of the styles".

Ireland

The Irish Parliament House in Dublin was the first building in the world specifically designed for a two-chamber legislature. It was also the first purpose-built Parliament of modern times to adopt a circular debating chamber.

By the eighteenth century its precursor, Chichester House, the location of parliamentary meetings for over 100 years, was badly decayed. The sum of £6,000 was allocated for the building of a new Parliament House, on the same site at College Green, close to the intellectual centre of Dublin, Trinity College. Captain, later Sir, Edward Lovett Pearce, designed the new Parliament, one of the first classical buildings in Dublin. Pearce, an amateur architect who

had probably worked for some years in the office of his cousin Sir John Vanbrugh, introduced Palladianism to Ireland.

The foundation stone was laid in 1728 and the building was substantially complete when Pearce died prematurely in December 1733. The original Parliament consisted of only the central portion of the present building. After the Act of Union with England (1801), the building was made redundant and subsequently became the home of the Bank of Ireland. The parliamentary chambers remain, but have been adapted to accommodate new functions: the former House of Commons being a banking hall and the former House of Lords serves as a meeting room.

Bank of Ireland Banking Hall
Site of the former House of Commons, right

Bank of Ireland West Hall
Site of the former House of Lords, centre

Exterior of Old Irish Parliament Building
Now Bank of Ireland, below

Henry Grattan urging
the claim of Irish
Right in the Irish
House of Commons,
1780
W.Hartnell & Co after
Francis Wheatley

Leinster House

Leinster House 2000
New parliamentary accommodation including offices and committee rooms by the Office of Public Works, Dublin

Leinster House is home to the Oireachstas or Irish Legislature. It accommodates the Dáil Éireann (the Irish parliament), Seanad Éireann (the Senate) and the Irish Presidency.

Leinster House is the largest and most notable eighteenth century town house in Ireland. Designed in 1745 by Richard Castle as the town residence of James FitzGerald, 20th Earl of Kildare, it was originally known as Kildare House until the 1760s when the Earl was raised to the Dukedom of Leinster. Castle, who had already been employed by the Earl's father to remodel Carton, Co. Kildare, the FitzGerald's country seat, had almost completed his work when he died in February 1751. The house was originally entered via a rusticated arch on Kildare Street demolished in the late nineteenth century to make way for the National Library and Museum.

The interior was largely completed by Isaac Ware who also designed the main staircase, the Supper Room (now the Library) and the entire suite of rooms overlooking Leinster Lawn. In 1775 the second Duke of Leinster employed James Wyatt to design the Picture Gallery (now the Senate Chamber).

In 1815 the third Duke sold Leinster House to The Dublin Society, later Royal Dublin Society. The Society constructed a 700-seat lecture theatre, which opened in 1897 equipped with electric lighting, an organ, a laboratory bench for practical demonstrations, and a cinematic projector. In 1922 the Minister of Finance, Michael Collins, took the decision to establish the Dáil Éireann in the Royal Dublin Society lecture theatre, while the Senate convened in part of the National Museum.

This unsatisfactory separation of the chambers was resolved two years later when the Office of Public Works negotiated the acquisition of the whole building for the sum of £68,000. The Victorian lecture theatre still houses the Dáil chamber, although considerable alterations have been made. For example, the seating capacity of the octagonal chamber was reduced to less than 200 and the floor level was raised.

Leinster House
The largest and most notable eighteenth century town house in Dublin has accommodated the Dáil Éireann since the 1920s

Stormont

In the wake of the establishment of the Irish Free State, the Government of Ireland Act of 1920 granted Belfast the status of a provincial capital to resolve the determination of Ulster Protestants to retain their link with the United Kingdom. Initially the government, which held its first full session in the City Hall on 23 June 1921, was housed in various temporary accommodation including the Presbyterian Church of Ireland. In the search for a permanent location three sites – Belfast Castle, Orangefield and Belvoir Park – were considered and rejected. The Stormont estate was up for sale and considered to be the ideal location; the fact that it lay beyond the city boundaries was quickly solved by redrawing the city perimeter to accommodate it.

Stormont House, originally built in 1830 for Rev. John Cleland and only later to become known as Stormont Castle after it was refashioned by a local architect in the Scottish Baronial style, had narrowly escaped demolition. Ulster's first Prime Minister Sir James Craig made it his official residence and it was subsequently used as offices. The government held a limited competition for the design of a new parliament building for the adjacent site which was won by Arnold Thornley of Liverpool with a Greek revival style entry which *The Builder* magazine felt provided the required level of "dignity associated with Parliament".

The parliament building was to be a gift of the London government to the province and constructed under the supervision of the Board of Works. Foundations were laid

for a Parliament flanked by two wings to house the ministries and crowned by a central dome, features that were too much for Stormont's budget. Forced to redesign, Thornley reduced the building to four storeys of masonry construction which still used 135,000 cubic feet of Portland stone for which the total bill amounted to £1.2 million. There is a notable lack of either Irish or British symbolism in the interior detailing all of which was strictly based on Greek classical motifs. The double height Commons Chamber and smaller Lords Chamber witnessed their first parliamentary session in 1932, the same year that Thornley was knighted for his work.

The Northern Ireland parliament was abolished by Westminster in 1973 and replaced by the first Northern Ireland Assembly, which met in a single chamber of seventy eight elected members. Within two years that too was dissolved and subsequently replaced by the Northern Ireland Constitutional Convention, elected in May 1975 and dissolved within a year. In 1995 a cataclysmic fire caused by an electronic fault in the control systems under the Speaker's Chair destroyed much of the building. The history of the place was deemed so central to the political heart of Northern Ireland that it was decided to rebuild the original, despite the fact that inadequate records of the details existed and a lengthy archaeological excavation was required to secure necessary data. And most recently with the formation of the National Assembly of Ireland the building once again fulfils its intended purpose as the centre of political power in Ulster.

Stormont
Palladian architecture inspired Arnold Thornley from Liverpool to create the monumental image of Stormont and determined the interior details, where there is a notable lack of either Irish or British symbolism

Commons Chamber and House of Lords
Witnessed their first parliamentary session in 1932. Thornley was knighted for his work at Stormont

United States of America

The United States of America's constitution designated a permanent home for the federal government in a district "not exceeding ten miles square". A rivalry between northern and southern interests resulted in a compromise location on the banks of the Potomac River. There the new capital city of Washington was laid out to Pierre Charles l'Enfant's masterplan.

In 1792 a competition for the design of the Capitol was won by William Thornton, an amateur architect, originally from Scotland. George Washington admired Thornton's neo-classical design for "its grandeur, simplicity and convenience" and five architects, including James Hoban, Stephen Hallet and George Hadfield, were appointed to implement Thornton's design. Professional rivalries resulted in the dismissal of Hallet and Hadfield, both accused of attempting to alter the original plan. Construction stalled until 1803 when the then President, Thomas Jefferson, appointed Benjamin Latrobe to continue the work. Jefferson wrote to Latrobe: "I think that the work when finished will be a durable and honourable monument to our infant republic, and will bear favourable comparison with the remains of the same kind of the ancient republics of Greece and Rome." The following year the Irish poet Thomas Moore described Washington as the "second Rome".

In 1814 the still unfinished Capitol was burned down by the British Army during the Napoleonic Wars. It was finally completed by Charles Bulfinch in 1826, thirty seven years after construction started. As the United States grew more space was needed and following an inconclusive architectural competition Thomas Ustick Walter was commissioned to expand the building. Walter more than doubled its size between 1851 and 1863 with the construction of the new House and Senate and the familiar cast iron dome.

One of the most widely recognised buildings in the world, the United States Capitol is synonymous with the American system of government. The democratic aspirations of the American people are represented in the classical design of the monumental building hailed as America's "Temple of Freedom".

Capitol
After its destruction
by the British,
24 August 1814

**Section and elevation
of the dome of the
US Capitol by Thomas
Ustick Walter**
Between 1851 and 1863
Walter more than doubled
the size of the Capitol
with the construction
of the new House and
Senate and the addition
of the cast iron dome

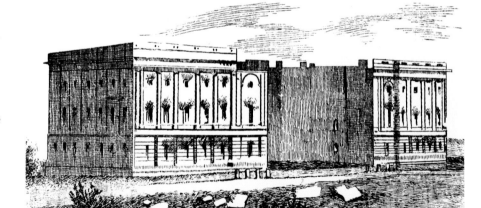

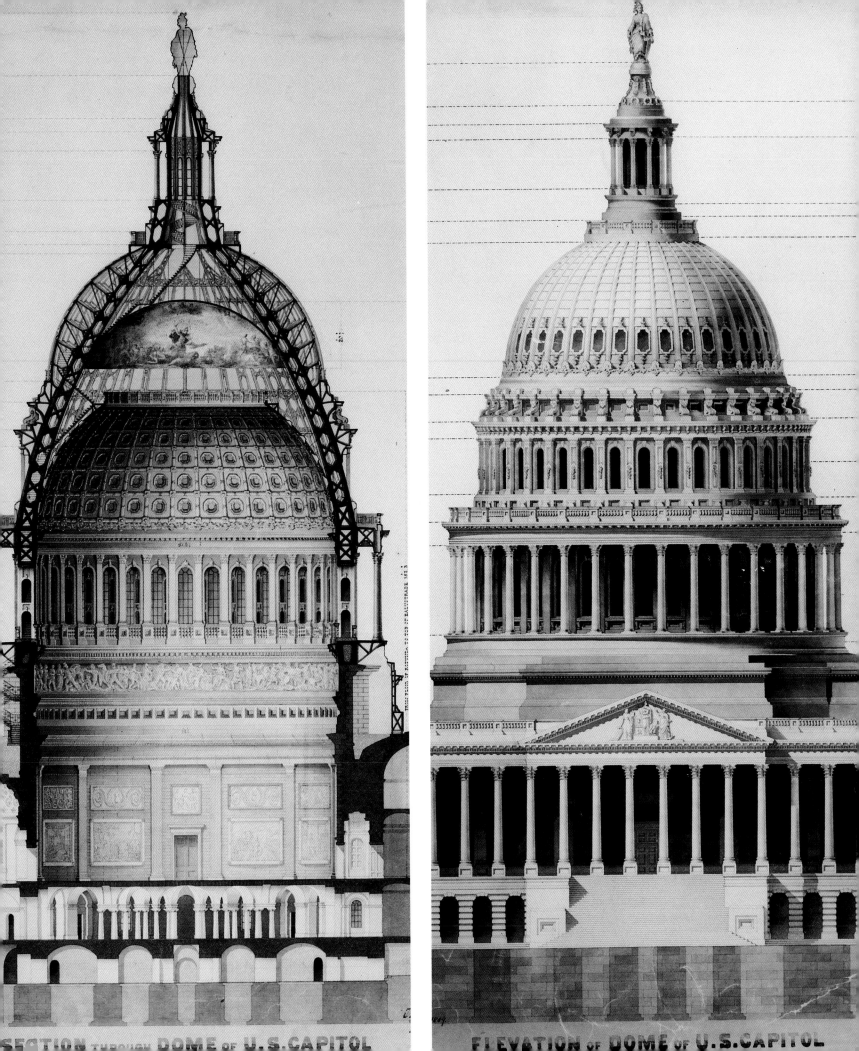

SECTION THROUGH DOME OF U.S.CAPITOL

ELEVATION OF DOME OF U.S.CAPITOL

India

The decision to relocate the seat of British India's government from Calcutta to the new imperial capital of New Delhi in the early twentieth century reflected a desire to make British rule appear to be more closely identified with Indian traditions. Calcutta was a European creation, Delhi had been not just a Moghul city, but also a much older urban centre for India. And at the same time a green field site outside old Delhi would escape the troublesome and politically radicalised climate of Bengal.

Sir Edwin Lutyens provided an overall conception for New Delhi and designed the Viceroy's House. From 1912 Lutyens collaborated on the project with Sir Herbert Baker, who had already built a Parliament for the Union of South Africa. At New Delhi

Baker was responsible for the secretariat buildings, legislative and houses for government officials. His aim was "to build according to the great elemental qualities and traditions, which have become classical, of the architecture of Greece and Rome, and to graft thereon structural features of the architecture of India as well as expressing the myths, symbols, and history of its people". But despite his original intention to make a pure classical structure, Baker was persuaded in the end to create a sophisticated synthesis of Western and Indian architectural motifs.

The chosen circular form raised concerns. In a letter to Baker of 1920 Sir William Marris, Home Secretary in the Government of India, expressed his reservations about

the design as he felt a circular colosseum did not adequately represent an expression of the parliamentary principles. As the building neared completion critics repeatedly compared it to a gasometer or bullring.

The Council House (now Parliament House) is a monumental structure occupying almost six acres of land, enclosed by an ornamental red sandstone wall with twelve entrance gates. Built from

indigenous materials and by Indian labour the massive circular edifice was designed to accommodate representatives of the three estates from the British colonial provinces and native principalities in three semi-circular chambers under one roof. The obvious alternative, a rectangular House, was deemed dangerous as it might encourage two-party government and foster divisions along strictly religious lines between Hindus and Muslims. The Legislative Assembly, designed for 400 members, was the simplest of the three chambers, while the Princes Chamber boasted the most opulent furnishings for its 120 members. Today, the two Houses of Parliament, the Lok Sabha (House of the People) and the Rajya Sabha (Council of the States), occupy two semi-circular chambers, the Princes Chamber now being the Library Hall.

The adoption of the British custom where a Member spoke from his seat in the House and therefore often has a number of listeners behind him caused acoustic problems. Baker addressed improved sound quality by lowering ceilings, installing convex facets in the teak panelling and installing acoustic tiles. The problem remained with various additional devices being employed to reinforce voices.

Finland

Finland's parliamentary buildings reflect
the self-conscious creation of a new
independent nation, emerging from
its past as an intermittent dependent of
Sweden and more recently of Russia. Whilst
still a province of Imperial Russia, Finland
opted for a unicameral parliament and
a session hall that could accommodate
a 200-member assembly. The building in
which the Diet of the Estates formerly met
and the House of Nobility were too small
for the new parliament when the country
finally received independence.

Eliel Saarinen won a competition to
design it in 1908, but his proposal for the
Parliament to be built on Observatory Hill
was never carried out. After the formal act
of independence two further architectural
competitions were held. The latter, despite
an entry by Alvar Aalto, was won by Johan
Sigfried Sirén whose proposal was submitted
under the motto "Oratoribus" (to the
Orators). The board's analysis of the winning
entry conveyed the spirit of the austere,
neo-classical design, describing it as a
"monumental cube" with a "stern outline".

The imposing facade of Kalvola granite
is dominated by fourteen columns crowned
with Corinthian capitals that illustrate the
influence of Sirén's detailed study of
classical architecture. The composition
of the Parliament House, rising above
the front steps to its elevated position,
represented classicism at its most
monumental.

The task of designing the Parliament
House as a forum of political power,
not as an office building for Members
of Parliament, was taken seriously by the
architect. One of the first considerations
to be decided was the seating arrangement
of the assembly chamber, designed around
the premise that the circular room was to
be twenty five metres in diameter. To ensure
the chamber reflected a modern European
design concept Sirén carried out a research
trip to look at the parliament houses in
Sweden, Denmark and Germany in November
and December 1925. By the time the
building was completed its 1920s style
classicism had given way to the pervasive
Modern Movement obsession with
functionalism, hence the proliferation
of tubular steel chairs in the interior
communal spaces. The building which
embodied the political and architectural
ambitions of several generations was
inaugurated in March 1931.

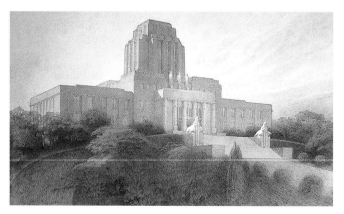

New Zealand

New Zealand's first parliament met in a wooden Gothic style building. It was destroyed by fire in 1907. In 1911 the government architect, John Campbell, and his assistant, Claude Paton, won a competition for the design of a new Parliament House with an Edwardian neo-classical building, which was officially opened in 1922.

At the heart of the building is the House of Representatives, based upon the oppositional layout of the British House of Commons. It contains rows of green leather seats placed two-and-a-half sword lengths apart exactly in the Westminster manner, with the exception of size and a slightly curved seating arrangement. The New Zealand parliamentary system, being derived from the British, contains many other symbols derived from the "mother of parliaments"; the Speaker's Chair was a gift from Britain and there is a replica of the British Mace.

The planned wing to the south of the main entrance was never built and it was almost fifty years before the executive wing, designed by Sir Basil Spence and known as the "Beehive", completed the complex. Spence was invited to lecture in New Zealand in 1964. A few days before his departure he was asked by the New Zealand High Commissioner in London to consider a design for the parliament buildings, which had stalled after many years of abortive schemes. Working on a small drawing board in his hotel bedroom, Spence produced the design in just two weeks. The circular building, rising from a rectangular podium, houses the Cabinet Room and ministers' offices. The final stages were completed by New Zealand's Ministry of Works in 1982.

The parliament of New Zealand currently occupies four buildings connected via a series of internal link-ways. The most recent addition to the parliamentary complex is Bowen House, a twenty two storey office block with apartments built in the later 1980s of reinforced concrete with a coated aluminium cladding system.

New Zealand Parliament
The 'Beehive' Executive Wing was completed in 1982

Sketch plan New Zealand Parliament extension, 1964
Sir Basil Spence

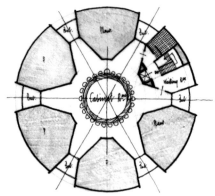

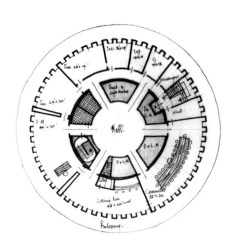

Line drawing, New Zealand Parliament extension, 1964
Sir Basil Spence

League of Nations, Geneva

The establishment of the League of Nations was conceived as an idealistic attempt to build the seat of a system of world government. In 1926 a competition was held to find an architect for the new building.

The jury members, chaired by Victor Horta, Hendrik Berlage, John Burnet and Josef Hoffmann, included a range of distinguished elderly architects; together they selected twenty seven designs from eight different countries and announced nine winners from 377 entries. Le Corbusier took part, but his design though recognised as of outstanding merit did not win the competition. It would have been a masterpiece, a synthesis of Le Corbusier's personal architectural language with a certain classical formalism. However his design was ruled out on a technicality – he had presented dyeline prints rather than the ink drawings stipulated. He campaigned to have the decision overturned, and later sued for damages, accusing the architects eventually appointed of plagiarising his plan. But the choice of which one to build was entrusted to a panel of five diplomats. Not one of the prize-winning entries was considered by those consulted to be suitable for execution and a compromise was reached: the French Swiss team of Henri Paul Nenot and Julien Flegenheimer were commissioned to produce a new design, together with the three other first-prize nominees (Giuseppe Vago, Carlo Roggi and Camille Lefevre).

The League of Nations complex on the beautiful site on the Lake Shore facing Mont Blanc was completed in 1937.

Aerial view
League of Nations
Built 1927-37

Extension to
League of Nations
By Sir Basil Spence, 1974

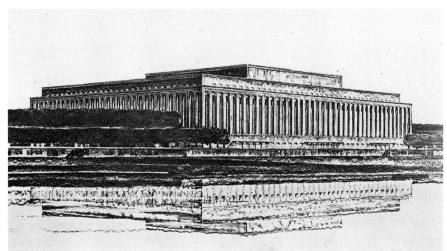

United Nations, New York

Le Corbusier was as frustrated by his experiences in the competition to build the headquarters of the League of Nation's successor, the United Nations, as he had been in Geneva. On 10 January 1946, twenty six years after the formation of the League of Nations, the United Nations Organisation opened the first session of its General Assembly. The Assembly, attended by fifty one member states, took place in Westminster Central Hall, London and was addressed by Prime Minister Atlee, who concluded that those "gathered in this ancient home of liberty and order ... must and will succeed". One of the first issues addressed by the General Assembly was the location of the permanent headquarters.

After various sites around the world were proposed, it was determined the new organisation's headquarters would be located in the United States.

The ensuing debate over whether the site should be urban, suburban or rural was finally resolved when the developer William Zeckendorf offered to sell a site on the East River, New York City. In 1947 John D. Rockefeller, Jr., purchased the options on the site for $8.5 million dollars and donated it to the United Nations. It was a spectacular case of enlightened self-interest. New York was able to stake a claim on the status of the capital of the world. A blighted area of the city was cleaned up. And the value of Zeckendorf's land holdings around the UN site shot up.

Architects called upon the United Nations to sponsor an international competition, but the organisation had no desire to repeat the mistakes of the League of Nations and no competition was held. Instead the diplomats appointed a group of leading international architects and invited them to design the complex collaboratively. It was a deliberate attempt to reflect the supranational collaborative ideals of the organisation. The following year an International Board of Design was formed and the group of architects from Europe, Asia, and North and South America gathered in New York to design the permanent United Nations Headquarters.

Wallace K Harrison (United States), Max Abramowitz (United States), Le Corbusier (France), Nikolai Bassov (Russia), Oscar Niemeyer (Brazil) and others were members of the advisory committee that devised the design during a four month period. Among his colleagues Le Corbusier was the dominant force and several of his concepts had a major impact on the final design, including the towering Secretariat and the wedge-shaped General Assembly. In one of the most elegant designs, Oscar Niemeyer proposed a vast open plaza, emphasising clearly articulated buildings. But it was Wallace K. Harrison, the Rockefeller's personal architect, who actually built the complex between 1947 and 1952.

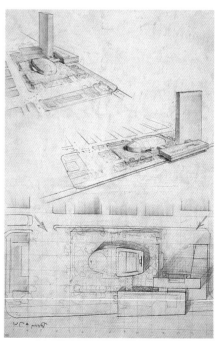

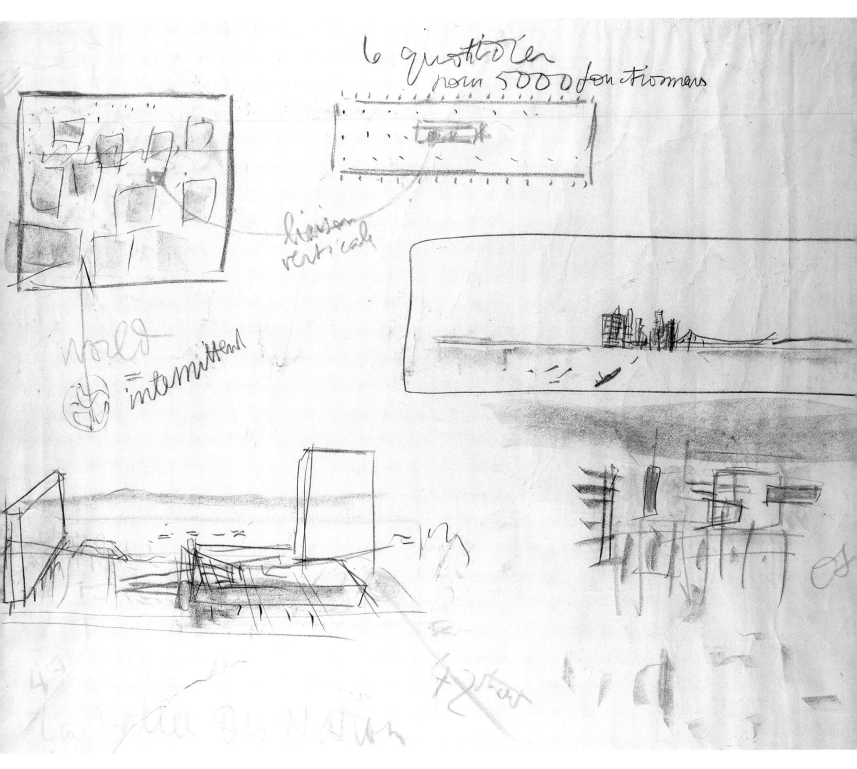

6 quartiers
non 5000 fonctionnaires

liaison
verticale

world
= intermittent

National identity through architecture

Chapter three

National identity through architecture

While democratic institutions have their origins in the classical city-states, a more direct ancestor is the European royal court. Parliaments were instruments of royal statecraft, a means for a ruler to secure the consent of his leading subjects. With the growth of the nation state, the role of parliament shifted, coming to predominate over monarchy as the expression of the national will. The architecture of the parliament building has been put to work in an attempt to express or reinforce this sense of national identity.

To follow the rise of national identity expressed through parliamentary architecture it is clear that if Athens provides us with the major precedent for the world's democratic traditions it is not the only one. Scandinavia offers another distinctive path. Iceland's Viking settlers established one of the Western world's earliest democratic societies based on an assembly, the *Althingi*, that met annually from around 930 AD. The Icelandic *Althingi* was unusual in that it united an entire country under a single legal system, without a monarch. The *thing* (voting assembly) was a democratic institution widely adopted throughout Scandinavia. Its offspring include the Isle of Man Tynwald, the annual assembly which met (and still meets) at the site of Tynwald Hill, a potent

national symbol created from soil gathered from the seventeen ancient parishes of the Isle of Man.

In the United Kingdom parliament developed from a council of nobles and high-ranking clergy that advised the early kings of England and followed the king around the country. After the Norman Conquest of 1066, this informal advisory group became a formal assembly known as the Great Council, which most frequently assembled at the Royal Palace of Westminster. By 1258 the barons led by Simon de Montfort, Earl of Leicester, appeared in arms at the parliament at Westminster, demanding the exclusion of all foreigners, and the appointment of a committee of twenty four members. Later that year a council of fifteen, with a baronial majority, was formed to advise the king, hence originating constitutional democracy as a governmental form. This model of a monarchy modified by other pressures representing significant property interests within the country can be seen in other European states, for example, the Polish Sejm which comprised a Senate and a House of Deputies from as early as 1493.

Alternative, non-classical traditions have been employed by nation states seeking to assert their own cultural diversity and through that their separate right to

existence under democratic government. Nationalism as a modern movement and ideology emerged in the latter half of the eighteenth century in Western Europe and America. During the nineteenth century the acceleration of popular nationalism, in the sense of national ambitions supported by mass electorates, required physical expression through assembly buildings in more and more countries as ancient empires such as the Austro-Hungarian began to break up. Bertrand Russell noted, "The new national monarchies in France, Spain, and England had, in their own territories, a power with which neither Pope nor Emperor could interfere. The national state, largely owing to gunpowder, acquired influence over men's thoughts and feelings which it had not had before, and which progressively destroyed what remained of the Roman belief in the unity of civilization."

In *Nations and Nationalism* Ernest Gellner defines nationalism as a "theory of political legitimacy" which holds that "the political and the national unit should be congruent".

By definition parliament buildings are expressions of the relationship between government and architecture. The buildings demonstrate faith in the cultural identity of a nation, serving two symbolic purposes simultaneously: acting as potent symbols of political power internally, that is to the

Canada's Parliament building at Ottawa
Depicted on banknote

Scotland's Old Parliament House, Edinburgh
Depicted on a Scottish banknote, opposite

people within a nation, and also providing an external example to foreigners of the confidence in that nationhood. Gellner recognised that the construct of national identity relied upon national historical continuity. Lawrence Vale observed in *Architecture, Power and National Identity* that "National identity .... is not a natural attribute that precedes statehood but a process that must be cultivated for a long time after a regime has gained political power." Historically culture and architecture have been used at the service of political and national ambition. Parliament buildings become monuments to national identity through their appropriation by the people of a particular nation. The cultivation of nationhood requires reinforcement and material representation.

Once the pressures for the establishment of parliamentary buildings had acquired significant momentum the process of commissioning these buildings had then to be undertaken. In Great Britain for example the new parliamentary structures were the result of a limited competition, restricted in the sense that only British architects were invited to provide designs in the specified Gothic or Elizabethan styles. The commissioning committee believed those styles best represented the aspirations of the British nation.

One contemporary architect, Charles Fowler, stated that the result of the competition would "in great measure determine the rank which the Arts of this country must take in relation to other civilised states" and *The Times* wanted to ensure "the erection of a noble Parliamentary edifice worthy of a great nation".

The success of this stylistic requirement is exemplified by the fact that the British Parliament continues to be known the world over as the "Mother of Parliaments", although in fact its architectural provenance, namely Gothic, originated in mainland Europe and is not specifically English. The Westminster model has subsequently been adopted both within the Commonwealth and beyond. The parliament buildings of Canada and Hungary, for example, both utilise the Gothic style. The desire to define national aspirations through appropriate architecture was further emphasised by the use of decorative ornament. Thus, although the external structures of these and other parliament buildings may have been copied from Westminster during the period of British dominance, national identity and political ambitions were satisfied through the application of indigenous architectural ornament such as flowers, animals and other types of decoration used both

externally and within the chambers.

Location also plays an important role. The selection of geographical location for the capital of a nation has been the subject of royal proclamation, tradition, or political decision.

Both the Westminster and Hungarian parliaments face the defining river of their respective cities, whilst Geoffrey Bawa, architect of the parliament of Sri Lanka, dredged a large swamp in order to create a floating parliamentary island. Charles l'Enfant laid out the city of Washington with the Capitol as its focus and over 150 years later Lucio Costa's masterplan for the new parliamentary city of Brasilia established the new political centre of the country. In spite of good intentions and immense effort architects and planners cannot determine the use of their structures. Bawa's romantic gesture has become a floating fortress for Sri Lanka, following a grenade attack in the assembly chamber, 18 August 1987. As nations themselves are constructed, sometimes parliament buildings fail to get off the drawing board. Bohdan Pinewski's scheme for rebuilding the Polish Sejm was realised only in part, his ambitious tower remaining only a sketch, and Josef Plečnik's gigantic plans for a parliament of Slovenia at Ljubljana was never built.

Iceland

If Athens is one root for the world's democratic traditions, Scandinavia offers another distinctive path. Iceland's Viking settlers established one of the modern Western world's earliest democratic societies based on an assembly, the *Althingi*, that met annually from around 930.

The *Althingi* continued to meet at *Þingvöllr* until it was disbanded in 1799. Within fifty years a royal decree issued in 1843 established a new *Althingi*. The following year elections were held and the consultative assembly of Iceland first met in 1845, initially in the Latin School in Reykjavik (now the Reykjavik Grammar School). In 1880-81 Danish architect Ferdinand Meldahl (1827-1908) designed the present building to house the

Icelandic *Althingi*. Built of hewn basalt, the Parliament House initially housed not only the *Althingi* but also three collections, the National Library, the Antiquarian Collection and the National Arts Gallery. The building was enlarged in 1908 and the "Rotunda" annex added.

The new Parliament House has also accommodated other requirements of the democratic nation state. The collections of books, antiques and works of art were moved in 1911 when the University of Iceland began life on the first floor of the present building. Since then the activities of the *Althingi* have outgrown the bounds of Parliament House and the parliamentary administration currently owns or rents several nearby buildings.

Althingi **House, the Icelandic Parliament building, designed by Ferdinand Meldahl, 1880-81**
Built of hewn basalt and located in gardens which serve as a reminder of the outdoor Viking assemblies from which Iceland's democratic traditions stem

Isle of Man

When Norse Vikings settled in the Isle of Man they brought with them the concept of an open-air assembly of freemen.

The earliest existing records of the ceremony describe the Tynwald of 1228, when a battle resulted in the death of the Manx king Reginald. The Isle of Man Tynwald had many features similar to those of the open-air Icelandic *Althingi*: a Law Hill, enclosed and surrounded by a green; joined by a pathway on the east to a Court House; and a place of worship, St John's Church. The twelve foot high Tynwald Hill, an artificial mound covered in turf, is believed to contain earth from all the seventeen ancient parishes. For more than two centuries a protective canopy has been raised over the topmost of four circular platforms during the annual assembly.

Engravings of the Tynwald Hill, 1774
The twelve foot high artificial mound is believed to contain earth from all the seventeen parishes of the Isle of Man

Tynwald Ceremony, 1998
Temporary structure erected for the ceremony, right

Poland

The Sejm, Poland's parliament, originated in 1493 when a national assembly was convened comprising a Senate and a House of Deputies. In the first centuries of its existence, during the period known as the Republic of Nobles, the Sejm was exclusively representative of the nobility. The Polish court at that time differed from its European counterparts because of the limitations placed on royal authority in favour of the wide-ranging powers of the Sejm. Parliament's membership, however, was confined exclusively to an elite. Plenary sessions were held in the halls of royal castles, initially in Krakow and later, after Poland's capital was transferred to Warsaw in the sixteenth century, in the Royal Castle.

When Poland regained its sovereignty after the First World War, the former secondary school, the Alexandrian-Marian Institute for Young Ladies, was adapted to function as the Parliament. On March 17, 1921 the first constitution in reborn Poland established a dual chamber parliament in keeping with the country's parliamentary tradition.

In 1925 the architect and curator at the Royal Castle in Warsaw, Kazimierz Skórewicz, was commissioned to extend the existing Parliament premises. Soon afterwards construction began, supervised

by Skórewicz, who paid attention to even the smallest detail and specified indigenous building materials. The single exception of one shipment of Belgian marble for tiling the inside walls of the Hall of Debate actually resulted in poor acoustics. Furnishings were designed by Steven Sienicki and the outside walls of the hall were decorated with a frieze of art-deco style stone reliefs by Jan Biernacki and Jan Szczepkowski, including those which symbolise the Army, Religion and Fine Arts. On 27 March 1928 parliament held its first plenary session in the new amphitheatre-shaped Hall of Debate.

The buildings were reduced to rubble during the Second World War. A bomb fell right through the middle of the Hall of Debate, yet the walls withstood the blast. Remains of the nineteenth century buildings and the oval edifice, which symbolises the Polish parliament, were quickly rebuilt. The Hall of Debate was covered with a twelve tonne dome put in place with the help of helicopters and this time its walls were covered in fabric. However, the still less than perfect acoustics demanded the installation of microphones.

Parliament needed more space and Bohdan Pinewski's design for expansion,

Hall of Debate
right

Sejm main entrance hall
centre

Staircase detail
The balustrade elements represent the architect's children, far right

Unbuilt project for parliamentary tower
Bohdan Pinewski,
1949-51, left

The Sejm
Hall of Debate and old
House of Deputies, right

approved in 1949, was mostly
completed by 1952. Pinewski's
idea for a central tower as a modern
national symbol in the composition
of parliamentary buildings was never
realised. Clear iconography of both
the nation and of the architect
was. Exterior stonework panels depict
birds and foliage and inside tapestries,
carvings and paintings depict figures
and scenes from Polish history. The
grandiose entrance hall is dominated
by a split staircase, with snake handrails
and images of the architect Pinewski's
daughters cast into the balustrades.

Canada

After the union of Canada's Eastern and Western provinces, a new capital was sought. Parliament had previously met at Quebec, Montreal, Toronto and Kingston. By 1857 the government, desperate to secure a permanent capital, but unwilling to decide such an issue in the political climate of the day, appealed to the Crown to intervene. On the advice of Sir Edmund Head, Canada's Governor General, Queen Victoria selected twenty nine rural acres on the Ottawa River for a "Westminster in the Wilderness". The small lumber town was a compromise location, making the role of the parliamentary complex of prime importance in establishing the new capital.

The following year a national competition called for buildings of a "plain substantial style of Architecture, of coursed hammer-dressed masonry, with neatly pointed joints, and cut stone quoins, window dressings, cornices and entablatures". The brief specified that the buildings be constructed with materials "found in the vicinity of the City of Ottawa".

Half the 32 identified competition designs were submitted by English architects. The first prize premium of £250 went to Fuller and Jones for their Gothic-style Parliament, and an equal sum to Stent and Laver for the flanking East and West Blocks, also Gothic in style. Although Fuller and Jones also submitted drawings and plans in the classical style as possible alternatives to their winning

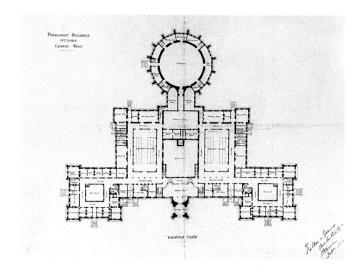

Plan, Parliament building, Ottawa
Fuller and Jones Architects, 1 February 1860

proposal they argued the Gothic style was superior and more suitable to the gently sloping site. Jones had little to do with the implementation of the design and Fuller was eventually appointed sole architect.

On 6 June 1866, the Province of Canada celebrated its first opening of parliament at its new capital. It was also its last. On 1 July 1867 the Province joined with New Brunswick and Nova Scotia to create the Dominion of Canada. With Confederation, the newly built parliament buildings became a symbol of nationhood. After a destructive fire, which spared only the Parliamentary Library (modelled on Smirke's design for the former British Library Reading Room in the British Museum), the Toronto firm of Darling and Pearson completed rebuilding the Parliament in 1920.

Parliament building, Ottawa
Queen Victoria selected the 29 rural acre site on the Ottawa River for the Canadian Parliament which she described as a "Westminster in the Wilderness"

Hungary

The underlying issue for Hungary's Parliament was its reflection of the status of Hungary within the Austro-Hungarian empire. The Budapest Parliament was built as a powerful architectural assertion of that distinctive identity.

The parliament building was the product of a competition of 1882. Following a number of unsuccessful competitions in the previous decade that competition attracted only twenty designs. Prizes were awarded to four architects (three of whom were Hungarian): Alajos Hauszamnn, Albert Schickendanz & Vilmos Freund, Otto Wagner of Vienna, and the winning design by Imre Steindl. Steindl, an apprentice stone-carver, who had studied architecture in Vienna and his native Budapest before becoming professor

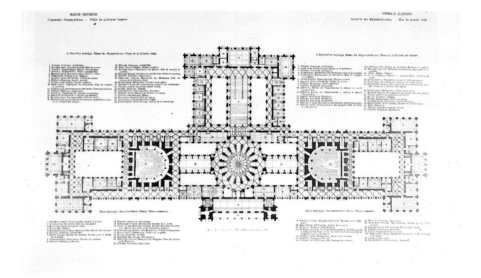

Commemorative book
Hungarian parliament
building, 1906
right, below

at the Technical University, dedicated the rest of his life to building his masterwork.

Steindl was well aware of the relationship between architecture and national identity: "I don't want to create a new architectural style for the parliament, because I could not build such a monumental building that has to stand for hundreds of years with ephemeral details. I have tried modestly and carefully, as is required by art, to bring a national and unique spirit to this magnificent medieval style." His design was an eclectic mix of old and new.

The exterior recalls the Palace of Westminster, both in composition and in the way it addresses its riverside setting. Indeed the Parliament surpasses Westminster in scale and grandeur; nearly 40 kilograms of gold was used for decorations, 90 statues

and the coats-of-arms of various cities and counties adorn the facades and the inner walls are adorned with 152 statues. Steindl's Gothic inspiration was combined with nationally specific references, such as stone carvings based on Hungarian plant types. Much of the building utilised Hungarian craft techniques and indigenous materials, resting upon a gigantic 2.5 metre thick concrete foundation.

The building, finally completed on 2 September 1903, was a massive undertaking employing an average 10,000 workers on site at any one time. Steindl who had directed work on site, even when he had to be carried there in a chair, died just five weeks before the building was first put to use.

**Hungarian Parliament
on the Danube**
The exterior of the
Hungarian Parliament
recalls the Palace
of Westminster, both
in composition and
in the way it addresses
its riverside setting

Slovenia

When Slovenia emerged from the former Yugoslavia as an independent state in 1991, it hurried to devise its own national insignia and currency. It chose to depict the architect Josef Plečnik on its banknotes, a tribute to the role he had played in creating a sense of national identity for a state that had never previously enjoyed an independent existence.

In the late ninteenth century, when Slovenia was an Austro-Hungarian province, Plečnik was a protégé of the architect Otto Wagner in Vienna. Later he moved to Prague, where the President, Tomas G. Masaryk, commissioned him to create a "democratic castle" for the new Czech state in 1925. Masaryk's brief to Plečnik was that he should give the castle the character of a residence of a democratic country. Indeed, Plečnik's career is marked by a belief in the ideal of democracy in architecture and the desire to create environments to serve the widest possible number of people. Returning home to Ljubljana, he worked on the design of a Parliament for Slovenia within the context of Marshal Tito's Yugoslavia in 1947. He proposed a "Cathedral of Freedom", the drawings for which demonstrate two of his favourite motifs, the cone and the inward leaning column. The monumental scheme did not meet with unanimous contemporary support and remains unbuilt, but with its mixture of fundamentalist geometry and classical detail, architecturally it is one of the most remarkable parliamentary projects of the twentieth century. For Plečnik it was the last in a series of proposals that represent his vision for Ljubljana as the Athens of Slovenia, most of them unexecuted.

Parliament of Ljubljana
Plan and elevation
of unbuilt design,
Josef Plečnik, 1947

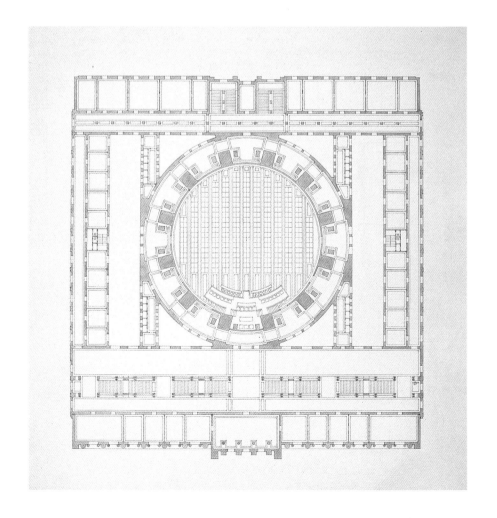

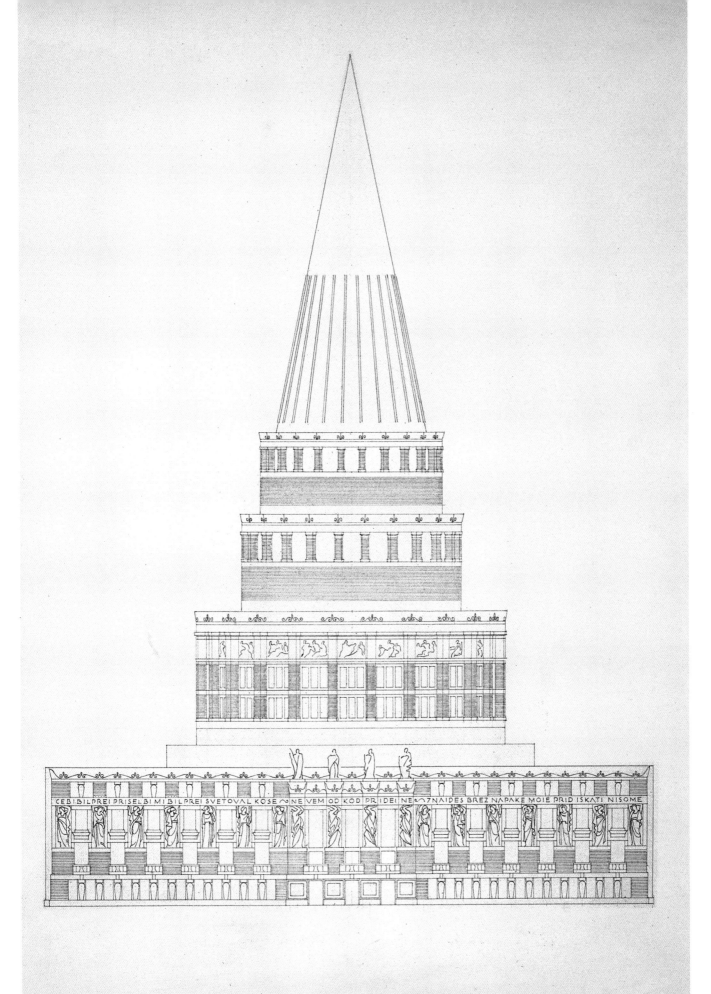

CE BI BIL PREI PRISEL BI MI BIL PREI SVETOVAL KO SE NE VEM OD KOD PRIDE I NE Z NAIDES BREZ NAPAKE MOIE PRID ISKATI NISOME

Sri Lanka

The parliament of Sri Lanka now meets at Sri Jayewardenepura, one of the country's ancient capitals. The new parliamentary complex was built under the initiative of Junius R. Jayewardene's United National Party. Despite a continuing civil war and a bitterly contested national identity, Jayewardene decided to build a new parliament building in 1979, 31 years after the island republic had achieved independence from Britain.

Geoffrey Bawa, an architect with a long record of synthesising vernacular traditions with a modern sensibility, was commissioned to design the new complex. Bawa suggested dredging to create an island site, located to the east of the ancient capital of Kotte, where the ruins of the old citadel overlooked a large swamp.

The resulting parliamentary complex is a series of copper-roofed pavilions which appear to float on a crescendo of terraces above the lake. There are references to classical precedents, to traditional Sri Lankan monastic architecture and to Kandyan temples, but the gridded rationality was wholly contemporary. The project took only three years from inception to completion. Due to the tight building schedule the initial design was developed in Bawa's small office with working drawings produced by the Japanese contractor Mitsui.

Bawa wanted to create a sense of accessible democracy, cultural harmony, continuity and progress, but that image has been compromised by the security cordon around the parliament complex. In August 1987, five years after its completion, the chamber was the target of a grenade attack by Tamil separatists which fatally wounded a Member of Parliament.

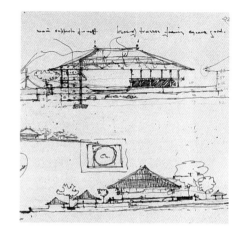

Parliament chamber
Five years after its
completion the chamber
at the heart of the
parliament complex
designed by Geoffrey
Bawa was the target
of a grenade attack

The making of Westminster

Chapter four

The making of Westminster

The Palace of Westminster is the best known building in the United Kingdom. It was specifically designed as an assertion of the national character of the nation. The rebuilding of the Houses of Parliament after the fire of 1834 was perhaps the most obvious example of the British state representing itself through architecture with the knowledge that it actually had a conscious stylistic choice to make. The two sets of green leather benches, set two-and-a-half sword lengths apart, serve to define parliament more than anything else, both architecturally and politically. When the House of Commons debated how best to rebuild itself after its chamber was destroyed in the Second World War, Sir Winston Churchill said, "The whole character of the British parliamentary institution depends upon the fact that the House of Commons is an oblong and not a semi-circular structure." This confrontational layout was the result of a series of historical accidents.

Britain's parliament developed from a council of nobles and clergy that advised the early kings of England. Parliament followed the king's court and consequently assembled in the Great Halls of royal residences around the country, most often at Westminster. After the Norman Conquest in 1066, this informal advisory group became a formal assembly known as the Great Council. It was the focus for a long drawn-out conflict between monarch, ministers and barons who more than once resorted to force to resolve their disputes. By 1265 the barons, led by Simon de Montfort, Earl of Leicester, had imposed a constitutional system that divided power

between the king and a parliament in which, along with the barons, bishops and abbots, sat four knights from each shire and two representatives from certain towns. Three electors appointed nine councillors who nominated ministers of state. This was the fullest representative assembly yet convened in England and can be regarded as the origin of the present system.

In 1547 parliament finally found a permanent home, at the site of the Royal Palace of Westminster in the capital. The palace was originally constructed as royal apartments, rather than as a meeting place of the national legislature. Canute the Great, a Danish king who ruled England by right of conquest from 1017 to 1035, was the first monarch to make his home at Westminster. After Canute's palace burned down, rebuilding was initiated by the Saxon king Edward the Confessor and was completed by his successor, William the Conqueror, who won the crown in 1066. Other sovereigns added to the buildings, which were once again destroyed by fire in 1512. Henry VIII abandoned the Palace of Westminster for York Hall, renaming it Whitehall, in 1529 and none of the succeeding monarchs used the palace as a residence.

The ancient palace of the English kings was a rambling conglomeration of buildings used, often indiscriminately, for a variety of purposes, ceremonial, judicial, financial and residential. The oldest and most dominant structure on the site was the medieval Westminster Hall, built in the 1090s by William Rufus. The twin towers either side of a centrally placed doorway were part of Richard II's remodelling of Westminster Hall in the 1390s, under the direction of Henry

Yevele and the master carpenter responsible for the present magnificent hammerbeam roof, Hugh Herland. By the mid eighteenth century, the facade of Westminster Hall was partly obscured by a ramshackle collection of coffee-houses and public houses (with the names "Hell", "Paradise" and "Heaven") which sprang up to provide refreshment for politicians, lawyers and visitors to the Hall. Westminster Hall was not only the site of the Law Courts but traditionally the setting for the Coronation Banquet.

The early meeting places of both the Peers and Commons at Westminster were crowded, makeshift and adapted from existing buildings. The House of Commons initially met in the Chapter House of Westminster Abbey, until the mid sixteenth century when Edward VI granted use of the medieval Chapel of St. Stephen. The Gothic Royal Chapel, built two hundred years earlier, was completed by Edward III on the ruins of the original St Stephen's Chapel. The seating arrangement at St Stephen's determined that members sat facing one another and the distinctive structure of the oppositional chamber was established. In order to prevent argumentative MPs drawing their swords and fighting each other in the House, the distance between the two front benches of opposing parties was established as two-and-a-half sword lengths apart. Due to its regal associations, the Peers or Lords chamber has always been more elaborate and ornate than the Commons, which is hung with the famous Armada tapestries. The monarch was placed at the centre of the chamber and seated on the throne.

The House of Commons, 1833
This painting by Sir George Hayter shows the galleries added by Christopher Wren to accommodate the extra 45 Scots Members of Parliament following the Act of Union

The complex of buildings at Westminster was subject to continual restoration and was refashioned on many occasions. In the eighteenth century Sir Christopher Wren gave an account of "the weakness and craziness of the House of Commons" warning that stormy weather could cause the roof to fall in. The fourteenth century clerestory and roof were removed and a new roof constructed at a lower level. At the beginning of the nineteenth century James Wyatt made amendments to both chambers. More ambitious remodelling schemes came to no avail. The most significant alterations were designed by Sir John Soane, Attached Architect at the Office of Works, whose Law Courts on the site adjoining Westminster Hall opened in 1826, but were ultimately demolished within sixty years.

In 1831 a Select Committee was appointed to consider the "possibility of making the House of Commons more Commodious and less Unwholesome". The Committee took evidence from a number of architects including Benjamin Wyatt, Sir Jeffry Wyatville and Sir Robert Smirke. Wyatville's suggestion of building a new House was accepted by the committee. Two years later Sir John Soane, Decimus Burton, Francis Goodwin and others put forward proposals for how this might be achieved. Suggestions were predominately in Gothic or neo-classical style. James Savage planned a circular chamber and Rigby Watson put forward an octagonal shape. William Kent's scheme, designed almost 100 years earlier, was also reconsidered. And a start was made on Soane's piecemeal remodelling of the approaches to the House of Lords. In 1834, however, fire created an opportunity to rebuild Parliament completely.

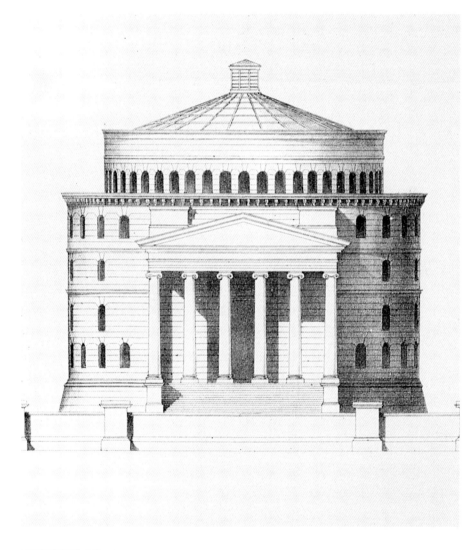

James Savage proposed a semi-circular House of Commons Chamber, 1831, above
Adam Lee, right
Francis Goodwin, centre
Rigby Watson, far right

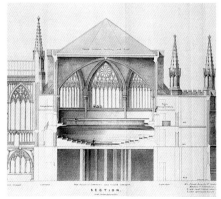

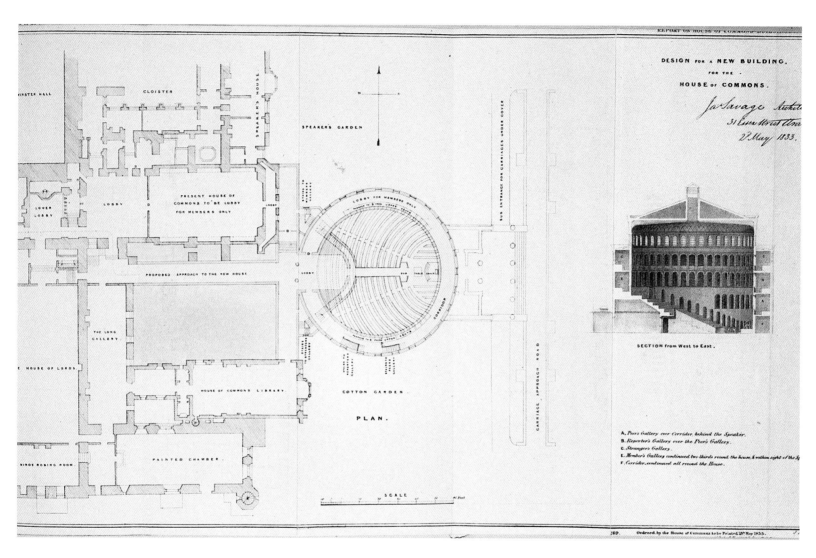

DESIGN FOR A NEW BUILDING.
FOR THE
HOUSE OF COMMONS.

Ja Savage Archt
31 Essex Street Strand
2ª May 1833.

SECTION from West to East.

A. Peers Gallery over Corridor, behind the Speaker.
B. Reporter's Gallery over the Peer's Gallery.
C. Strangers Gallery.
E. Member's Gallery continued two thirds round, the house, & within sight of the Sp
F. Corridor continued all round the House.

WESTMINSTER HALL
CLOISTER
SPEAKER'S HOUSE
SPEAKER'S GARDEN
PRESENT HOUSE OF COMMONS TO BE LOBBY FOR MEMBERS ONLY
LOBBY FOR MEMBERS ONLY
LOWER LOBBY
LOBBY
PROPOSED APPROACH TO THE NEW HOUSE
SUB ENTRANCE FOR CARRIAGES UNDER COVER
THE LONG GALLERY
HOUSE OF LORDS
HOUSE OF COMMONS LIBRARY
COTTON GARDEN
CARRIAGE APPROACH ROAD
PLAN.
KINGS ROBING ROOM
PAINTED CHAMBER.

SCALE

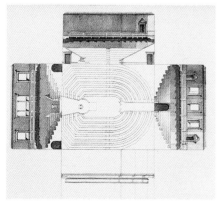

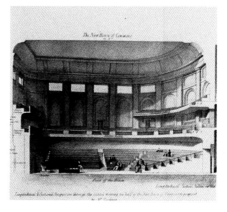

Designs submitted to the Select Committee appointed in 1831 to consider the "possibility of making the House of Commons more Commodious and less Unwholesome"
James Savage, top
Copy of plan by William Kent, dated 1799, left
Francis Goodwin, centre and right

**The Burning of the
Houses of Parliament,
1834**
J M W Turner
Amid thousands
of onlookers, the future
architects of the new
Houses of Parliament
Charles Barry and
A W N Pugin watched
the dramatic fire

**Competition designs
for the New Houses
of Parliament, 1835**
William Railton
Thomas Hopper
David Hamiliton

There have been numerous fires at the Palace of Westminster, but none as dramatic as that of the night of 16 October 1834, when the Houses of Parliament were devastated. The fire was caused by builders' overloading furnaces in the House of Lords with wooden tally-sticks. As the ancient medieval buildings were being consumed by flames, all efforts were directed towards saving the Great Hall. The tall, thick stone walls provided an excellent barrier against the spread of fire and the building survived. Amid thousands of onlookers, Sir Charles Barry and Augustus Welby Northmore Pugin both observed the dramatic scene. Pugin remarked, "There is nothing much to regret and a great deal to rejoice in. A vast amount of Soane's mixtures and Wyatt's heresies have been effectively consigned to oblivion. Oh it was a glorious sight to see his composition mullions and cement pinnacles and battlements flying and cracking."

The fire came at a time when the idea of rebuilding the Houses of Parliament was already in circulation and suggestions of arson were raised. The old Houses were cramped, ill-ventilated and inconvenient and there is little doubt that the devastation of the old Palace of Westminster gave British architects their finest opportunity since the Great Fire of London.

A new Palace of Westminster was not the inevitable consequence of the fire. Immediately after the old palace was destroyed King William IV offered the nearly finished Buckingham Palace for parliament's permanent home. Parliament rejected the idea on the basis of its location, considered even less fashionable than Westminster. And they were troubled by the fact that the Royal Palace would have required vast alteration for legislative use. Lord Melbourne's administration and the Whig

First Commissioner of Woods and Works called in Robert Smirke, the architect of the British Museum and attached to the Board of Works. Smirke organised temporary accommodation for both Houses (the main contract for which was given to his brother-in-law) and drew up a modest scheme, which was approved by the king and the Prime Minister Sir Robert Peel (who employed Smirke on his private building works).

News of Smirke's involvement and general criticisms of recent official architecture prompted fury in the press and the *Spectator* took up the theme, demanding that a design should be obtained by "a competition, open to all, foreign as well as native artists". It was felt that public competition alone could identify the best architect's abilities and express the common belief in the virtues of a competitive society.

On 9 February 1836 the House of Commons approved the appointment of a Select Committee to consider and report on such "Plan as may be most fitting and convenient for the permanent accommodation of the Houses of Parliament". Their first consideration was the critical issue of location, as it was said the site on the banks of the Thames was unhealthy. The committee was divided. Joseph Hume thought it would be better to remove the Houses of Parliament to a more open location such as Marlborough House or St James's Palace or to a new building behind the National Gallery. Mr Kearsley MP felt the present site to be extremely inconvenient and an alternative should be found. Sir Robert Peel however argued that the currents of air induced by the tide were healthy and advocated "the retention of a site with which were associated many of our most glorious historical associations". He also refuted the objection that the Houses of Parliament were too remote from the residences of the Members by suggesting it was an advantage, "inasmuch as it not only insured them exercise, but the House an attendance, which, in all probability, could not be obtained if their residences were close at hand".

Hume advocated a new building and supported the idea of open competition. In a letter to Peel, Tory MP Sir Edward Cust recommended a limited competition to be judged by "a commission of unpaid gentlemen interested in architecture". At this stage Peel's minority government was in no position to impose its will on the issue and despite the Prime Minister's distaste for open competition, a national competition was duly organised. Contemporary architect Charles Fowler recognised the result of the competition would "in great measure determine the rank which the Arts of this country must take in relation to other civilised states".

On 3 June 1835 the committees on rebuilding for both Lords and Commons announced a joint policy for an architectural competition. Anyone could submit a design for the new Houses of Parliament that met the following conditions: the Gothic or Elizabethan styles were specified and drawings were to be submitted at a scale of 20 feet to one inch (chosen because it happened to be the scale of Smirke's plans) with no coloured or perspective drawings, within four months. There was no direction for how the chambers should relate to each other, although it was expected that the Commons chamber should retain its oppositional form, and no budgetary requirements were set.

Fearing professional jealousy, the Government elected to employ members of the Royal Commission rather than architects to judge the 97 submitted entries. Lord Duncan, the Minister responsible for nominating the commissioners, under the chairmanship of Charles Hanbury Tracy MP, was surprised that some of those nominated declined to act, including Lord De Grey, first president of the Royal Institute of British Architects, who was engaged in the rebuilding of Wrest Park. The final decision lay with Parliament.

The results were announced at the end of February in 1836. First prize was awarded to Charles Barry, second to Chessler Buckler, third to David Hamilton and fourth to William Railton. The aggrieved losers criticised the competition process, on the basis that four months was too short a time to submit designs (indeed Francis Goodwin died, reportedly following the stress and exhaustion of preparing his submission to meet the schedule) and for the restriction to the prescribed Gothic or Elizabethan styles. Despite its popularity later in the nineteenth century few of the designs submitted were in the Elizabethan manner, which Charles Barry described as "an incongruous mixture of two styles in their decline, thus being utterly unworthy of the character of a great national edifice". *The Gentleman's Magazine* described the winning entry as "a Grecian design overlaid with Gothic ornament". In fact Barry's ingenious plan is classical in form and it was largely due to his collaborator Augustus Welby Northmore Pugin, whose expert knowledge of medieval Gothic architecture informed their design, that Westminster looks as it does. Pugin was a highly skilled draftsman who produced drawings for two of the competition entries: the fashionable Scottish architect James Gillespie Graham's as well as the winning

scheme. Pugin seems to have been unmoved by Barry's victory in the competition and the announcement went unrecorded in his diary.

In April 1836 competition entries were exhibited at the National Gallery, with the exception of Barry's winning scheme, which was not unveiled publicly until May as it was withheld for use by parliament. Criticism of the competition process from the architectural community was further inflamed by restrictions on architects who wanted to visit the exhibition. Public opinion, however, backed the choice of Barry. Sir Robert Peel sympathised with Barry's difficult position, stating he "had firmly made up his mind – never again to act as a Commissioner upon any subject of this kind, where a preference was to be given to the skill of one man as compared with that of others who had entered into competition upon the same work … But … he would rather be a Commissioner than the successful competitor, to be hunted and pursued with every species of invective in the way that Mr Barry had been. If the consequence of successful competition were to be exposed to such a series of attacks as those which had been directed against that gentleman, he – Sir Robert Peel – would infinitely rather remain in privacy and oblivion."

Peel questioned the brief's vagueness about budget, to which the Chancellor of the Exchequer confirmed, "No limitation whatsoever with respect to expense was contained in those resolutions … the Commissioners were empowered to take nothing into consideration besides the beauty and convenience of the plans laid before them for selection." Hume felt that the House had made serious errors in the competition process, particularly as Charles Barry had exhibited his plan publicly before the decision of the Commissioners in

its favour. Peel, however, rejected Hume's proposals that the process be started again. Even in opposition Peel was Barry's most powerful advocate, yet Hume remained his most persistent critic.

At the age of forty Barry was already an accomplished architect with a prospering practice carrying out commissions in both Renaissance and Gothic styles, most notably the Gothic revival King Edward VI Grammar School, Birmingham (1833), for which Pugin had prepared 127 drawings. Contrary to Barry's expectations, building the New Palace of Westminster did not see the number of commissions in his office rise. Indeed, in 1849 Barry reported quite the opposite: "I have been obliged to give up more than two-thirds of a lucrative practice and have to my knowledge been deprived of employment to a very considerable extent from a prevalent feeling which has existed that it was out of my power to attend to any other work."

In April 1836 Barry responded to the Committee's questions about budget and schedule, estimating the building would take six years, but he was still working on the foundations in 1842. The process of building the Parliament while the workings of government continued proved to be a massive and time consuming task. Parliamentary committees became deeply embroiled in such issues as the selection of stone. The prolonged delays were in part due to parliament, which obliged Barry to make several changes in his plan, and also led to a masons' strike. In addition Barry's perfectionist nature and struggle to create the perfect elevation, with its roof line dominated by three towers: King's Tower (as the Victoria Tower was then known), the Clock Tower and Westminster Hall, meant the project was to occupy him for the rest of his life.

Pugin also laboured tirelessly on the project, producing a plethora of design drawings in his own hand, for he employed no assistants. Following the successful competition submission Pugin executed the estimates drawings for Barry and then ceased his connection with the project until 1844 when Barry asked him to help with the considerable work of designing the wealth of Gothic detailing and furniture of the many interiors. Even while the project was underway their collaboration led to competing claims for both Pugin and Barry to be credited as the real author of the new Houses of Parliament. The issue was taken up by both men's sons. E. Welby Pugin published a pamphlet in 1867 that asked, "Who Was the Art Architect of the Houses of Parliament?" His aim was to ensure "that my father should receive his fair share of that fame which is now wholly accorded to one, who has hitherto been regarded as the sole designer of that which my father mainly originated". Alfred Barry retaliated in his own pamphlet published as a counterblast: "Every architect, in conducting works on a great scale, must necessarily avail himself of assistance in detail." Barry must be credited with being the architect. It was he who controlled the overall composition. Pugin, however, had the strongest impact on the decoration.

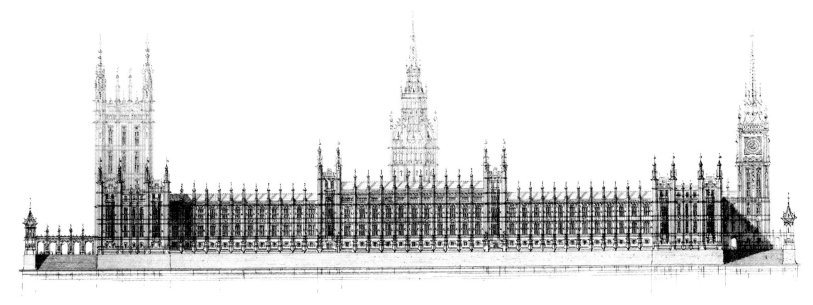

North Front, contract drawing
Sir Charles Barry worked on his composition in order to perfect the location of the towers, 1840, left

River Front, intermediate drawing
1840, below

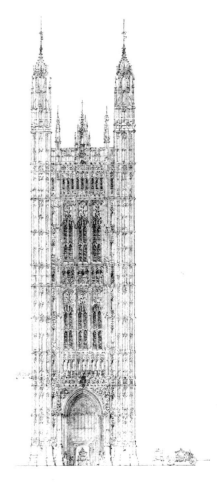

King's Entrance Tower,
elevation
A W N Pugin, 1835, top

Elevation, ground
plan and section,
King's Entrance Tower,
estimates drawing
A W N Pugin, 1836-7,
right

Interior furnishings,
House of Commons,
including Speaker's
Chair, estimates drawing
A W N Pugin, 1836-7,
top opposite

House of Peers,
internal furnishings
Charles Barry, based
closely on A W N Pugin's
estimates, c.1841,
bottom, opposite

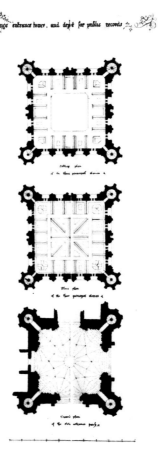

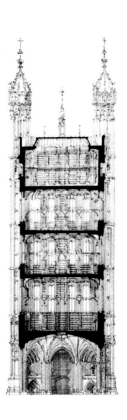

Plan shewing Ceiling of One Compartment of Division Gallery.

Elevation of One Compartment of Division Gallery.

(All Mouldings ½ full size)

Speaker's Chair (Front)

Side Elevation

Plan

The Upper end of House shewing Speaker's Chair

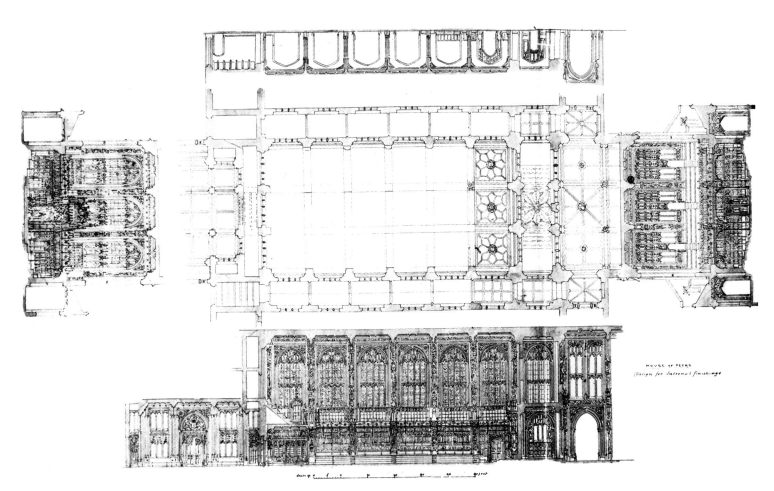

HOUSE of PEERS
Design for Internal finishings

The first stone was laid on 27 April 1840. The House of Commons chamber eventually opened in 1850, and the building was finally completed in 1870, ten years after Barry died.

That the chamber was too small to seat all its members at the same time was not Barry's fault. He was asked to provide seats for only 428 of the 658 members. More disturbing was the fact that the chamber's acoustic performance was so poor that in the early days debate was almost impossible. A new ceiling was hung, but after this alteration the architect, "no longer considered the House his own work", and, according to his son "would never speak of it or enter it, without necessity".

By the time the project was finished in 1870, the revived Perpendicular Gothic fashionable in 1835 had fallen out of favour with refined taste and the New Palace was for a time condemned as a stylistic travesty. Eighteen years after completion the House was regarded as so inadequate that a Select Committee was appointed to consider what should be done. Charles's son Edward Barry proposed that a new House should be built.

In fact nothing was done until World War II, when the House of Commons was destroyed by a direct hit from a bomb on the night of 10 May 1941. While considering its reconstruction, some members proposed building a modern interior within the burnt-out Gothic shell. But they were no match for Winston Churchill's rhetoric. "We shape our buildings and afterwards our buildings shape us," he told the House. "We have learned not to alter improvidently the physical structures which have enabled so remarkable an organism to carry on its work of banning dictatorships within this island and pursuing and beating into ruin all dictators who have molested us from outside."

Churchill outlined the two most crucial characteristics of the House of Commons: "The party system is much favoured by the oblong form of chamber. It is easy for an individual to move through those insensible graduations from Left to Right but the act of crossing the Floor is one which requires serious consideration ... The second characteristic of a chamber formed on the lines of the House of Commons is that it should not be big

enough to contain all its members at once ... If the House is big enough to contain all its members, nine-tenths of its debates will be conducted in the depressing atmosphere of an almost empty chamber."

Parliament accepted Churchill's argument for working with the spirit of Barry and Pugin's design for the House of Commons and Sir Giles Gilbert Scott was chosen as architect. In a Select Committee report, Scott summarised his intentions: "Feeling as we do that modernist architecture in its present state is quite unsuitable for the rebuilding of the House of Commons and bearing in mind that the chamber forms only a small portion of an existing large building, we are strongly of the opinion that the style adopted should be in sympathy with the rest of the structure."

Scott promised to remedy the "lifeless" Gothic detail of the old chamber, "with the result that, though still Gothic in style, the effect will be entirely different". The chamber, opened in 1950, maintains a more than superficial resemblance to the Barry and Pugin interior. But Scott's design is more restrained with ornamental oak detail restricted to bands between plain sections.

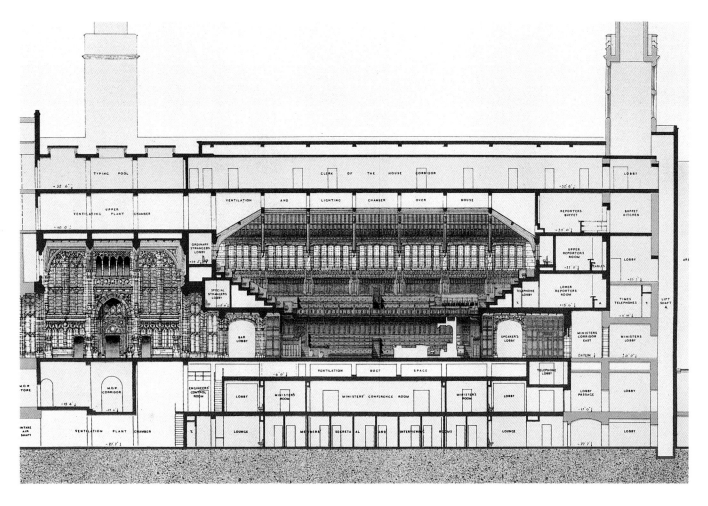

Section through House of Commons Chamber, 1944
Sir Giles Gilbert Scott's design maintains more than a superficial resemblance to the Barry and Pugin interior, following Churchill's statement, "We have learned not to alter improvidently the physical structures which have enabled so remarkable an organism to carry on its work ..."

**The Palace of Westminster,
Westminster Bridge and
Portcullis House**
Barry and Pugin's building
was designed for a very
different incarnation
of parliamentary
government. The need
for additional office space
has been addressed by
the recently completed
Portcullis House by
Sir Michael Hopkins

Modern Westminster

The rapid translation of Members of Parliament from part-time members of a gentleman's club into full-time professionals came increasingly to exercise Westminster. Ordinary members had no office space let alone room for assistants or researchers. Parliament needed an office block to accommodate them.

The accommodation shortage, the product of a parliament in which MPs were expected to maintain a career outside the House and operate from the corridors and the lobbies, would not go away. In 1965 Sir Leslie Martin had produced a plan to create a new government precinct in Whitehall that would have involved wholesale demolition of the Victorian ministries, but fierce opposition from the preservationists put an end to the scheme. In 1970 a new parliamentary building was proposed for a site facing the River Thames on Bridge Street, across the road from Big Ben. The government staged a competition and first prize went to Spence and Webster for a steel and glass box design. This time modernism won. Spence and Webster's design was a Miesian steel and glass structure that shocked some MPs. The design included a vast open courtyard with giant television screens to relay parliamentary debates to the public, a roof garden, and an escalator link to the House of Commons. The scheme would have been as radical as a Pompidou Centre transplanted to the centre of London. It proved too much for parliamentarians, but was killed off as much by the economic crisis of 1973 as for aesthetic reasons. However, government did acquire the site, on the river between Scotland Yard and Big Ben.

Competition entry,
section and
visualisations
Spence Webster, 1972-73

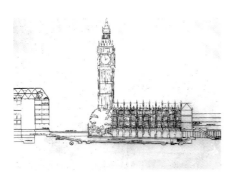

Photomontage of roof level and public forum
Winning competition entry for the extension to the Palace of Westminster, Spence Webster, 1972

With the Palace of Westminster bursting at the seams, MPs still needed office space, even though the Spence and Webster project had been abandoned. Sir Hugh Casson was brought in to produce a less controversial alternative, one that would pander to the cautious tastes of parliamentarians, and smooth away any embarrassing charges that the MPs were interested only in feathering their nests at the voters' expense.

Casson Conder presented a feasibility study in 1983 that carefully deferred to its neighbours. The scheme incorporated the facades of most of the original buildings on Bridge Street, providing new but undistinguished offices behind them. The first phase was opened in 1990 – the first purpose-built parliamentary accommodation since 1950. The second phase, which would have been executed by Ramsay Tugwell, was not implemented. The climate had swung back towards bold architectural statements.

Parliament Square
View of Bridge Street, showing before and after Casson Conder scheme for parliamentary office building
Top 1979, below 1991

**Proposal for New
Parliamentary Building**
Sir Hugh Casson and
David Ramsay, Casson
Conder Partnership, 1979

When it became clear that Westminster's Underground station would need rebuilding as part of the Jubilee Line extension a more ambitious architectural approach was decided on. Sir Michael Hopkins' design for courtyard offices crowned by a series of circular heat exchangers was selected in 1992.

Hopkins' scheme is contemporary in its detail, but reflects the decorative architecture of Norman Shaw's Scotland Yard in its silhouette. The building aspires to a visual and functional connection between the old and the new. Hopkins describes the aim of the project as the creation "of a building that will sit comfortably in its historic setting whilst at the same time providing all the facilities and energy efficiency expected of a later twentieth century building". It has involved complex engineering to accommodate new tube lines and platforms in its deepest levels.

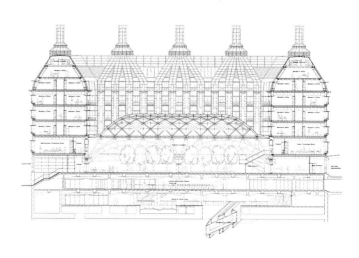

New parliamentary building, Bridge Street, Westminster
Cross section through offices and covered courtyard, Sir Michael Hopkins and Partners, 1995

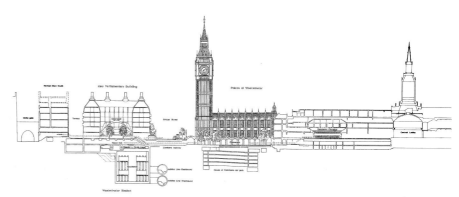

Portcullis House by Sir Michael Hopkins and Partners
After a quarter of a century the need for additional office space on the Bridge Street site has been fulfilled. Spence and Webster's modern vision was killed off, the retreat to the past with Casson Conder was implemented only in part, and at the start of the twenty first century Sir Michael Hopkins and Partners have completed the new office building for Members of Parliament

Commonwealth Parliaments

Commonwealth Parliaments

1 **United Kingdom**
Houses of Parliament,
Westminster

2 **Northern Ireland**
Houses of Parliament,
Stormont

3 **Isle of Man**
Legislative Buildings,
Douglas

4 **Jersey**
The States Chamber,
St Helier

5 **Canada**
Houses of Parliament,
Ottawa

6 **Ontario**
Parliament Buildings,
Toronto

7 **Quebec**
Parliament Buildings

8 **Nova Scotia**
Province House, Halifax
(in which Legislative
Assembly meets)

9 **New Brunswick**
Legislative Building,
Fredericton

10 **Manitoba**
Legislative Building,
Winnipeg

11 **British Columbia**
Parliament Buildings,
Victoria

12 **Prince Edward Island**
Province Building,
Charlottetown
(in which Legislative
Assembly meets)

13 **Saskatchewan**
Legislative Building,
Regina

14 **Alberta**
Legislative Building,
Edmonton

15 **Newfoundland**
House of Assembly,
St John's

16 **Australian
Commonwealth**
Houses of Parliament,
Canberra

17 **New South Wales**
Parliament House,
Sydney

18 **Victoria**
Parliament House,
Melbourne

19 **Queensland**
Parliament House,
Brisbane

20 **South Australia**
Parliament House,
Adelaide

21 **Western Australia**
Parliament House, Perth

22 **Tasmania**
Parliament House, Hobart

23 **New Zealand**
Parliament Buildings,
Wellington

24 **Union of South Africa**
House of Parliament,
Cape Town

The Westminster parliamentary model was exported to the Commonwealth, in terms of the exterior architecture of the buildings, the bicameral system and the paraphernalia of government. Particular items developed specifically for the Palace of Westminster, such as the Speaker's Chair and the Mace, were also used in most Commonwealth parliamentary chambers.

In June 1953 on the occasion of the Queen's Coronation a commemorative book entitled *Parliamentary Buildings of the Commonwealth* was commissioned by the Commonwealth Parliamentary Association. This is the photographic record it included, presented in the same order and format as the original publication.

25 India
Parliament House,
New Delhi

26 Bombay
Council Hall,
Bombay

27 West Bengal
Legislative Building,
Calcutta

28 Pakistan
Constituent
Assembly House,
Karachi

29 East Bengal
Legislative Building,
Dacca

30 Ceylon
House of
Representatives,
Colombo

**31 Southern
Rhodesia**
House of
Parliament,
Salisbury

32 Malta
Grand Master's
Palace, Valetta

33 Bermuda
House of Assembly,
Hamilton

34 Bahamas
Legislative
Buildings, Nassau

35 Mauritius
Government House,
Port Louis (in which
Legislative Assembly
meets)

36 Jamaica
Headquarters
House, Kingston
(in which Legislative
Assembly meets)

37 Barbados
Legislative
Buildings,
Bridgetown

**38 Trinidad
and Tobago**
Red House, Port
of Spain (in which
Legislative Assembly
meets)

39 British Guiana
Public Buildings,
Georgetown (in
which Legislative
Assembly meets)

40 Grenada
York House,
St George's (in
which Legislative
Assembly meets)

41 St Lucia
Legislative Council
Chambers, Castries

42 St Vincent
Court House,
Kingston (in which
Legislative Assembly
meets)

43 Dominica
Court House, Roseau
(in which Legislative
Assembly meets)

**44 British
Honduras**
Government
Buildings, Belize
(in which Legislative
Assembly meets)

45 Gold Coast
King George V
Memorial Hall, Accra
(in which Legislative
Assembly meets)

46 Nigeria
House of
Representatives,
Lagos

47 The Gambia
Government House,
Bathurst (in which
Legislative Assembly
meets)

48 Sierra Leone
The Secretariat,
Freetown

**49 Northern
Rhodesia**
Legislative Council
Building and Central
Government Offices,
Lusaka

50 Kenya
Memorial Hall,
Nairobi (in which
Legislative Assembly
meets)

51 Singapore
The Victoria
Memorial Hall
(in which Legislative
Assembly meets)

**52 Federation
of Malaya**
The Council
Chamber,
Kuala Lumpur

The modern supplants the classical

The modern supplants the classical

No century has seen the construction
of more parliamentary buildings than
the twentieth century. The wars and
revolutions, the constant shifts in the
balance of global power, the life-and-death
struggles of old and new nations are
measured out in a series of architectural
monuments, or would-be monuments. The
challenge for contemporary architects has
been to find ways of putting the vocabulary
of modernism to work in creating buildings
that reflect national aspirations.

Many of the major figures of twentieth
century architecture worked on new
Parliaments intended to reflect national
aspirations as well as the universal ideals
of the modern movement.

**Sketch of the
Acropolis of Athens
by Le Corbusier, 1923**
The political legacy
of Ancient Greece
is recorded in its
architectural monuments
which have inspired
many twentieth
century architects

Brasilia

For almost a century the Brazilian constitution contained a clause committing the country to move its capital from coastal Rio de Janeiro, the creation of the Portuguese colonists, to a new city in the interior. It was a pledge to create a Brazil that had ended its dependent relationship with the European colonial power.

The young mayor of the city of Belo Horizonte, Juscelino Kubitschek, was so impressed with the work of Oscar Niemeyer that he commissioned him to build the Pampulha complex – a church, hotel, restaurant, ballroom and yacht club around a lake on the outskirts of the city. Later, when running for president, Kubitschek promised apparently on a whim to obey the constitution and construct a new capital city and parliament complex if elected. Kubitschek conceived of the new city as a way of developing the vast and empty plains of Brazil. The project finally got underway and Niemeyer was appointed as chief architect of the new capital.

In 1956 a national competition allowed just eight months to masterplan the new city of Brasilia. Lucio Costa won the commission to plan his country's new capital. The resulting plan resembles a bird or aeroplane as Costa rejected the traditional grid and organised his plan along two main axes.

At the heart of the capital the Square of the Three Powers contains the Parliament Complex; described by Niemeyer as follows, "The Congress, exhibiting its main hierarchical sectors on the main contrasting bowls; the Ministry of Justice, with its falls pouring water, as in a miracle, through its front windowpane; and the Pantheon, enriching the horizon of the Three Powers Square, like a white bird". Niemeyer hoped that Brasilia "will be a city full of happy men, of men who feel life in all its fullness and fragility. Men, at last, who understand the value of pure and simple things – a gesture, a word of tenderness and solidarity."

Limited to a single term in office Kubitschek wanted the city to be constructed at speed to commit his successors irrevocably to the project. On 21 April 1960 Brasilia became the official capital of Brazil. In 1964, after a military coup, Niemeyer as a Communist was interrogated by police and placed on an unofficial blacklist, effectively barring him from federal building projects.

In 1986 Brasilia was recognised as a UNESCO World Monument and remains hailed as a monument to modernist urban planning despite practical difficulties with some of the buildings and their relationship to the rest of Brazil. Brazil's MPs still tend to leave for their constituencies on Thursday nights.

Sketch of National Congress Complex
Oscar Niemeyer

Masterplan
Lucio Costa, 1956

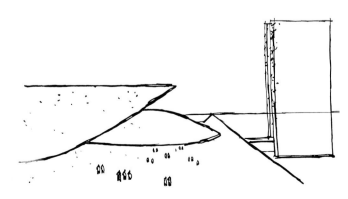

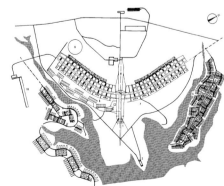

Brasília by Oscar Niemeyer, 1956-60
Kubitschek's vision of a new capital city, realised by Costa and Niemeyer, is hailed as a monument to modernist urban planning and recognised as a UNESCO World Monument in 1986

Chandigarh

Chandigarh was the product of post-colonial partition. When India and Pakistan were divided, so was the Punjab, and with the old administrative capital on the Pakistani side of the frontier, India had to build a new state capital. Prime Minister Nehru initially selected the architect Matthew Nowicki, a young Polish American, but he died in a plane crash before he could start work. Jane Drew and Maxwell Fry from London were asked to take on the project, and suggested that Le Corbusier be invited to design the monumental heart of the new city, while they retained responsibility for Chandigarh's residential areas.

This was Le Corbusier's most complete attempt to build a city. He was criticised for taking insufficient notice of the way in which Indian urban life is lived in the street, but his design nevertheless resulted in one of the most poetic and powerful realisations of architectural modernity put to work to create a democratic institution.

The capital was laid out as a series of buildings and monumental plazas, each of which is a defined entity. The major Capitol Complex consists of a progression of spaces and buildings that culminates in the Place of Assembly, a U-shaped office block with a massive front portico and what has been referred to as its "democratic roof".

Chandigarh, 1951-62
Le Corbusier's most
complete attempt to
build a modern city

Drawing of the Assembly
building by Le Corbusier,
1955, below

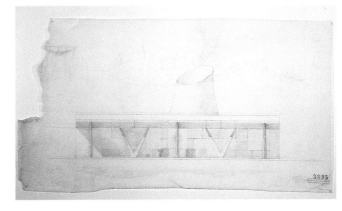

Dacca

Louis Kahn was formally appointed to design the new Parliament in Dacca at a time when Bangladesh was still politically linked to Pakistan, and before a bloody civil war transformed what had been known as East Pakistan into a new state.

In 1962 Muzharul Islam urged the Pakistani Department of Public Works to proceed with plans for the design of a new parliamentary complex. Three eminent architects were considered, namely Le Corbusier, Alvar Aalto and Louis Kahn. Kahn was formally appointed to design the National Assembly building in January 1964.

Kahn believed in the special nature of assembly, whether for religious or secular purposes, feeling that people "came to assemble to touch the spirit of commonness". His Parliament complex is a seven-storey structure comprising masses of different shapes, for different functions; a central 300 seat assembly chamber, surrounded by offices, a prayer hall and other ancillary spaces. Entrance to the assembly, at the north end of the building, and to the prayer hall, at the south end, is made via monumentally scaled plazas of brick.

Kahn died before the scheme was completed. Yet, despite the protracted genesis of the project, and the mismatch behind the liberal ideals underpinning the building and the often brutal nature of political life in Bangladesh, Kahn's dignified monumental brick structure, well suited to the conditions of the developing world, succeeds as a poignant piece of architectural sculpture. Construction was completed after Kahn's death by David Wisdom and Associates.

Dacca, 1962-1983
Kahn's parliament complex at Sher-e-Bangla Naga is a seven storey structure comprising masses of different shapes for different functions, including a 300 seat assembly chamber

Sketch for National Assembly Chamber by Louis Kahn, opposite

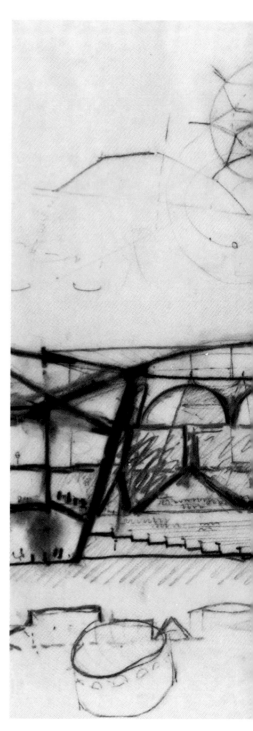

Parliament House, Canberra

Canberra, Australia's federal capital, is a city especially created for the purpose of government. Its location was selected so as not to favour either Sydney or Melbourne at each other's expense.

Walter Burley Griffin won the competition to lay out the city in 1912. Australia's provisional Parliament House, opened in 1926, was an exercise in restrained classicism that was functionally redundant by the 1960s. Its replacement, selected through another international competition, was completed in time for Australia's bicentennial in 1988.

The brief spelt out Australia's determination for a building that would have the symbolic resonance of Westminster or Washington. In 1980 the American architect Romaldo Giurgola, in partnership as Mitchell/Giurgola and Thorp, won the project with a design for a building that springs from the landscape, a building that is both monumental and accessible.

Parliament House, Canberra 1980-1988
Mitchell/Giurgola and Thorp created a new Parliament that grows out of the landscape, rather than being set as a monument upon it

The Hague

Pi de Bruijn's extension to the Dutch Parliament in The Hague is embedded within the context of a former royal palace that had already been remodelled over the years. They are a reflection of a Dutch response to history combined with the need for a modern home for Dutch democracy.

A competition held in 1977 to develop the Tweede Kamer was aborted at the end of 1978 when the jury concluded that none of the 111 entries was of sufficient quality. Three architects, including de Bruijn, were asked to prepare a plan for a newly appointed management team. The team in charge of the review refrained from making a decision and during the interim the scope of the project was being reconsidered. The final decision was to appoint de Bruijn's practice de Architekten Cie rather than select a scheme and to further review the options for development of the parliament site.

De Bruijn's design, completed in 1991, adopts a deliberately low-key architectural vocabulary – a reflection perhaps of the antipathy of the Dutch state to pomp and ceremony. Its public spaces are calculatedly democratic and informal; intimate, rather than monumental.

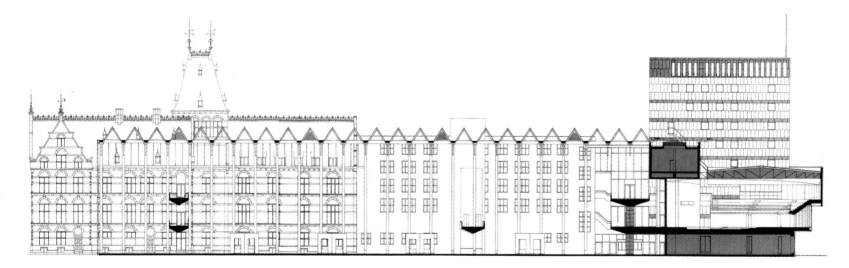

Bonn

The German Federal Republic chose the small town of Bonn on the Rhine for its Parliament, focusing post-war Germany westwards, away from the tensions of the eastern frontier.

Günter Behnisch and project partner Gerald Staib started work on the parliament complex in 1983. The Parliament was only completed in 1992, by which time the German state was on the edge of reunification, casting the future of the building in doubt. Bonn reflected Germany's attempt to exorcise its authoritarian past: this was a government of openness and accessibility, rather than intimidation. The open organisation was literally represented in the transparency of the glass walls, which allowed strong connection between the building and the surrounding landscape, particularly the Rhine.

In 1999 the Bundestag moved back to Berlin in the refurbished Reichstag and the building at Bonn lost its status as national Parliament.

Berlin

No parliament building is more charged with historical significance than Berlin's. Originally completed in 1894, Kaiser Wilhelm's baroque-style Reichstag was designed by Paul Wallot after a protracted competition. Later it became the seat of the Weimar Republic.

The Reichstag's destruction by fire in 1933 marked Germany's descent into totalitarianism. It was here that the Red Army unfurled the hammer and sickle to mark the end of the Second World War. During Germany's partition the shattered structure was left to rot, eventually stripped of the surviving period detail and converted into a utilitarian convention hall and exhibition space. The Reichstag's adoption as the Parliament for a reunified Germany in the 1990s was a highly symbolic act, narrowly carried in a debate in the Bonn parliament.

Following a competition in 1992, Sir Norman Foster was chosen as architect to turn the old Reichstag into a new parliament building befitting Europe's most powerful state. Initially he envisaged the Reichstag as the centrepiece of a great public space, sheltered next to the Spree beneath a broad steel and glass roof. Cost forced a different strategy, in which the presence of a new chamber is marked by a transparent cupola containing a public viewing gallery. Foster described his mission to transform the Reichstag, "the reconstruction has been conceived as a way of transforming a famous national monument, full of melancholy and stirring memories, into an optimistic symbol both of the new Germany and the new Europe".

New parliament building
Foster and Partners turned the old Reichstag into a new parliament building befitting Europe's most powerful state

Winning competition scheme, 1992, below left

Theatres of democracy: European Parliaments

Each democratic assembly reflects, at least to a degree, the national characteristics represented by the assembling delegates.

In England that style and temperament was thought best served by a rectangular chamber fitted with tiered, opposing benches two-and-a-half sword lengths apart. Other nations have preferred semi-circular chambers.

The German photographer Jörg Hempel has photographed most of the parliament buildings in Europe both inside and out. His series of images of the debating chambers illustrates the architectural differences between the unicameral and bicameral systems of government.

11 Dublin, Ireland
Architect – Richard
Castle, 1745-1748

**12 House of Commons,
Rome, Italy**
Architect – Bernini, 1653
Adaptation by Carlo
Fontana, 1694

13 Senate, Rome, Italy
Architect – Michelangelo,
designed mid 16th
century
Completed mid 17th
century

**14 Luxembourg,
Luxembourg**
Architect – Charles
Arendt, 1858-1881

**15 The Hague, The
Netherlands**
Architect – Pi de Bruijn,
1980-1991

16 Lisbon, Portugal
Architect – Baltazar
Alvarez, 16th century
Reorganisation in 1834

17 Madrid, Spain
Architect – Marcisco
Pascul y Colomer,
1843-1850

18 Stockholm, Sweden
Architect – Avon
Johansson, 1894-1906
AOS arkitektkontor,
1975-1983

19 Moscow, Russia
Architect – D N Chechulin,
P P Shteller and others,
1965-1981

20 Oslo, Norway
Architect – Emil Victor
Langlet, 1857-1866
Alterations and additions
by Nils Holter, 1949-1959

The Welsh Assembly

The Welsh Assembly

The devolutionary impetus, in its architectural expression within the United Kingdom, begun by the commissioning of the Scottish Assembly in Edinburgh, continued in March 1998 when the Welsh Office announced a design competition to select an architect for the Welsh National Assembly.

The former prime minister Lord Callaghan led the design assessment panel which selected the architect of the new Welsh Assembly by means of a two stage competition process. The panel selected a shortlist of six firms from those who submitted interest in the project and invited them, for an agreed payment of £8,000, to produce a design proposal and fee bid.

In his foreword to the brief Lord Callaghan offered the following opinion:

"This competition offers the Architectural profession the opportunity to express a concept of what form should be assumed by a democratic Assembly listening to and leading a small democratic nation as we enter the next millennium. It will not be overly adversarial in shape or in argument, although there will be strong regional interests and differing priorities.

The Panel will welcome innovation but not unproven experiment, and environmental factors will be taken fully into account. The Chamber must be an effective place of debate, and the building should create a welcoming impression to those who work in it and to the many who will visit it. In due course, we would dare to hope it will become a visible symbol, recognised and respected throughout the world, whenever the name of Wales is used."

On the 5 October 1998 the following six shortlisted firms submitted schemes.
• Benson and Forsyth
• Itsuko Hasegawa Atelier
  with Kajima Design Europe
• Eric Parry Architects
• Richard Rogers Partnership
• MacCormac Jamieson Prichard
• Stride Treglown

After considering all six schemes and interviewing the designers Lord Callaghan speaking for the design assessment panel said "The presentations were outstanding from a world-class set of design teams."

The winner of the competition by unanimous vote was the Richard Rogers Partnership.

The special merits of the submitted scheme noted by the panel were simplicity, straightforwardness, elegance and economy. The Rogers scheme allowed for "light and transparency and will provide generous open spaces".

In Callaghan's view, the design represented the "open modern democracy" that the Welsh Assembly ought to be. The successful practice, the Richard Rogers

Partnership, thus took on the responsibility of creating the most important public building in Wales.

The location for the new Assembly had been the subject of considerable debate with various sites including Swansea Guildhall, Cardiff City Hall and even the idea of a mobile assembly based on the idea of travelling Eisteddfods (proposed in *Touchstone, the Magazine for Architecture in Wale*s). Perhaps the most popular alternative was the refurbishment of Cardiff City Hall, one of the prominent buildings in the capital. In 1997 the then Secretary of State for Wales, Ron Davies, explored the possibility of purchasing this historic building. However, the Council refused to accept the £3.5 million offer made for the long lease.

The decision having been taken to locate the Assembly in the capital it was decided to make it the centrepiece of the Bay area that is now being rapidly regenerated. The site faces out to sea and the world beyond, a physical expression of Wales' new political confidence and self-belief.

Rogers's scheme responds directly to the challenge of the site. The building comprises a public plaza firmly anchored to the water's edge, stepping upwards and into the site, enclosing the administrative functions beneath it.

With this commission the Richard Rogers Partnership scheme aims to symbolise democracy by encouraging participation in the democratic process facilitated by the creation of an open and publicly welcoming building. In response to the client's demand for the architecture of the building to express openness and transparency, the central idea of the new Assembly building is to attempt to make the democratic process more accessible. Under an undulating lightweight roof, sheltering both internal and external spaces, the building is entirely transparent at the public level, while the administrative level is private and the aspect is onto quiet courtyard spaces.

The Assembly Chamber has been designed to accommodate the sixty elected members and seating arrangements are suitable for an inclusive and participative elected body. The design of the chamber also takes into account the increasing importance of television broadcasts of debates to the people of Wales and beyond.

Another central criterion for the building is that the Assembly itself is the "first political body in the United Kingdom to have an obligation to promote sustainable development". The concept of sustainability is easier to assert than to realise, and the architecture of the building will go a long way to give true meaning to this idea.

The scheme is due for completion October 2003.

Cardiff

Richard Rogers Partnership Manifesto
for the National Assembly for Wales

"We propose a building that:
• Symbolises democracy by encouraging
  public participation in the democratic
  process
• Is accessible because it is easy to
  understand
• Makes visible the workings of the
  Assembly
• Creates spaces with the minimum
  of walls and corridors
• Provides a protective environmental
  envelope
• Reduces energy consumption
  by maximising use of daylight
• Engages with, and is open to
  its surroundings
• Is a flexible concept that can
  accommodate change
• Is made secure by good planning
• Is a concise expression of the new
  institution
• If the people occupy the building then
  it will assume symbolic significance
• A people place = a successful assembly
  building"

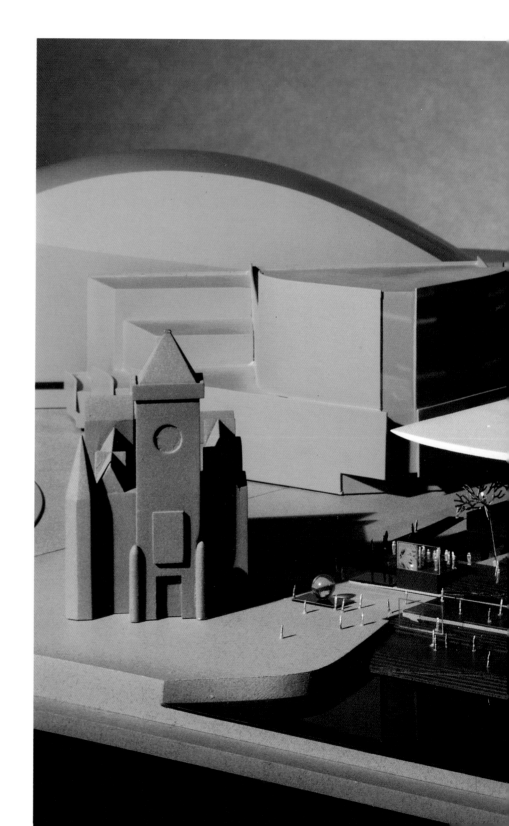

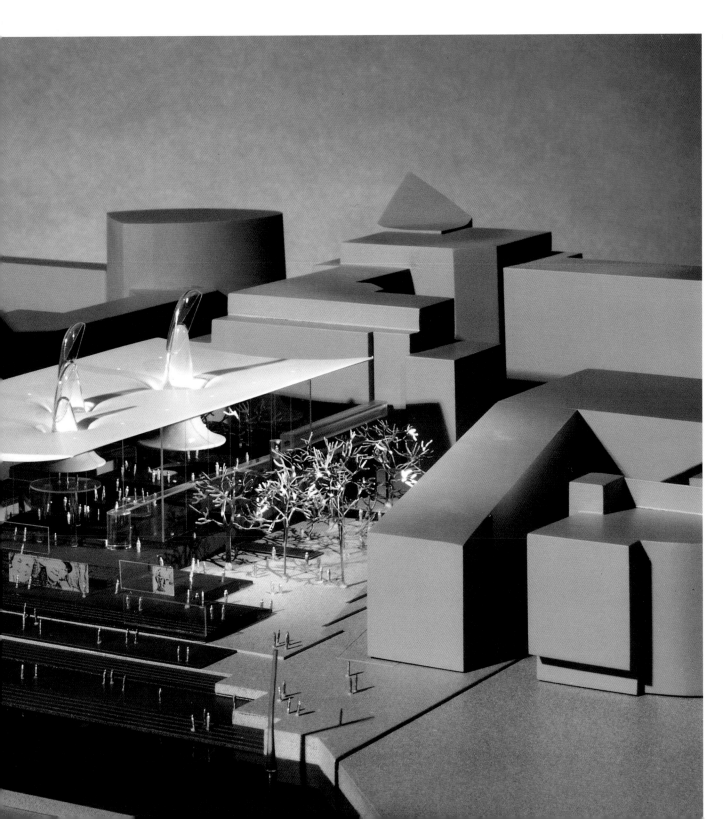

Competition model
Richard Rogers
Partnership

Cardiff

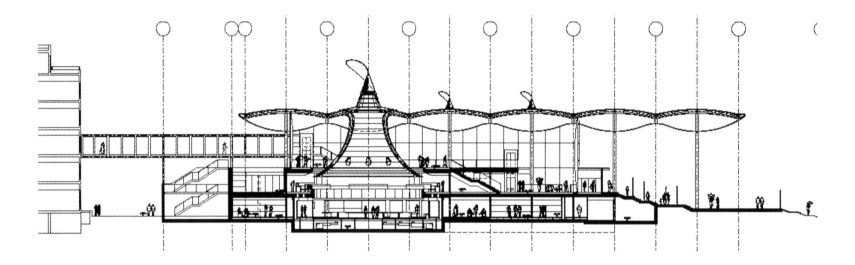

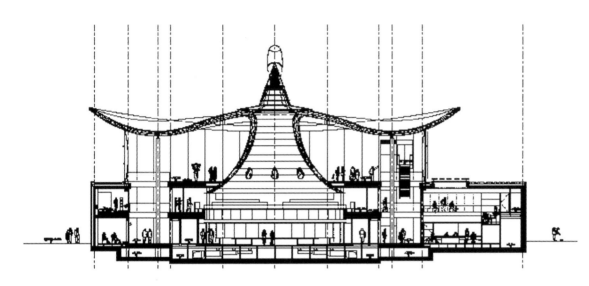

Welsh Assembly
Sections by Richard
Rogers Partnership

Sectional model, below

Cardiff

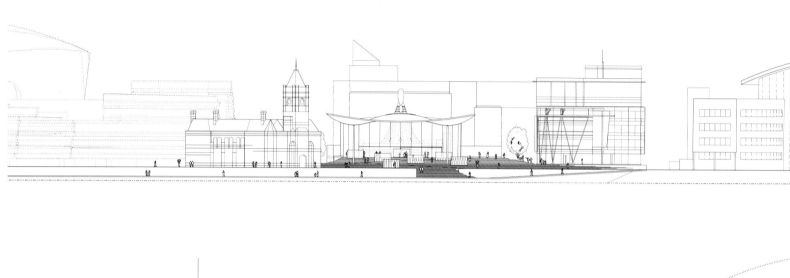

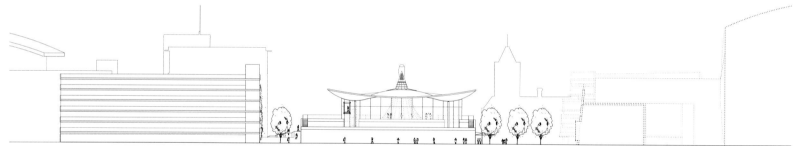

Welsh Assembly
Elevations by Richard
Rogers Partnership, left

**Visualisation of the
Welsh Assembly**
Located next to the
Pier Head building as
the centrepiece of Cardiff
Bay's redevelopment,
above

The origins of Scotland's Parliament

The origins of Scotland's Parliament

For the first time in 300 years Scotland has its own parliament, with a new permanent home in Edinburgh. Tradition, of course, was an important factor in the choice of architecture and of site, but so was the wish of contemporary Scotland to show its openness and innovative spirit. The new Scottish parliament building, designed by Enric Miralles, and selected after an international competition, will do justice to that spirit.

Scotland's democratic traditions date back to ancient times. Open air assemblies played a vital part in the ceremonial practices of early Scottish kingship. In its early days Scotland's parliament followed the monarch's court and convened at a variety of locations including the Abbey at Scone and at Perth, Stirling, Linlithgow and Holyrood, before settling in Edinburgh. Between 1489 and 1513 both Parliament and the Court of Session met in the cramped space of the new Tolbooth, Edinburgh, next to St Giles. In 1632 Charles I, unsatisfied with available accommodation, demanded that a new building be provided.

The most important event of the political calendar was the opening of parliamentary sessions, marked by a ceremony known as the "Riding of Parliament". A seventeenth-century engraving shows the customary procession of the members of parliament from Holyrood Palace to Parliament House. Drawn by Roderick Chalmers it probably shows the calvacade of 23 April 1685, depicting the burgesses followed by commissioners of the shires and nobility. Next in the colourful spectacle came the regalia of Scotland, trumpeters, pursuivants and heralds with the Lyon King, and then the King's Commissioner and his entourage.

When the members arrived at Parliament House the Commissioner was received by the Lord High Constable and the Earl Marischal who escorted him to the throne, in front of which the regalia were laid. After a sermon the Three Estates, the nobility, clergy and burgesses, got down to business.

Woodcut of the Arms of Scotland
Thomas Davidson, Edinburgh, 1540

Parliament House
In the upper part of the Kirkyard of St Giles, situated on Edinburgh's ancient spine, the Royal Mile, detail from James Gordon's Map of Edinburgh, 1647

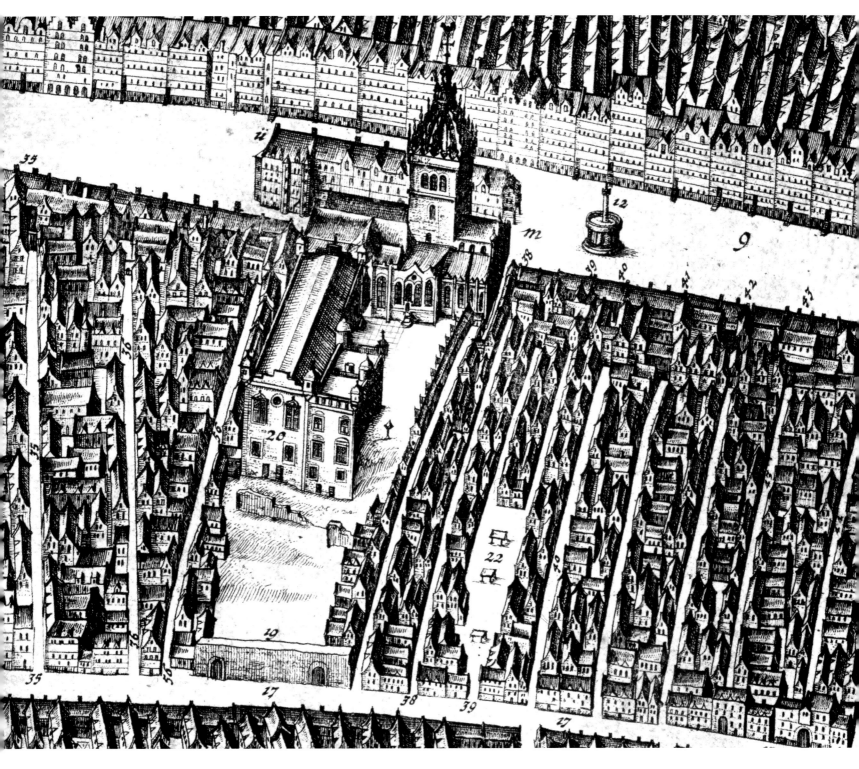

Two mounted trumpeters, with coats and banners, bare headed.
Two pursuivants in coats and foot mantles, ditto.
Sixty three Commissioners for burghs on horseback,
two and two, each having a lackey on foot;
the odd number walking alone.
Seventy-seven Commissioners for shires,
mounted and covered, each having two lackeys on foot.
Fifty-one Lord Barons in their robes, riding two and two,
each having a gentleman to support his train,
and three lackeys on foot, wearing above their liveries velvet coats
with the arms of their respective Lords on the breast and back
embossed on plate, or embroidered in gold or silver.
Nineteen Viscounts as the former.
Sixty Earls as the former.
Four trumpeters, two and two.
Four pursuivants, two and two.
The heralds, Islay, Ross, Rothesay, Albany, Snowdon, and Marchmont,
in their tabards, two and two, bareheaded.
The Lord, Lyon King at Arms, in his tabard with chain,
robe, baton and foot mantle.
The Sword of State, born by the Earl of Mar.
The Sceptre, borne by the Earl of Crawford.
The Crown
Borne by the Earl of Forfar.
The purse and commission, borne by the Earl of Morton.
The Duke of Queensberry, Lord High Commissioner,
With his servants, pages, and footmen.
Four Dukes, two and two.
Gentlemen bearing their trains,
and each having eight lackeys.
The Duke of Argyle, Colonel of the Horse Guards.
A squadron of Horse Guards

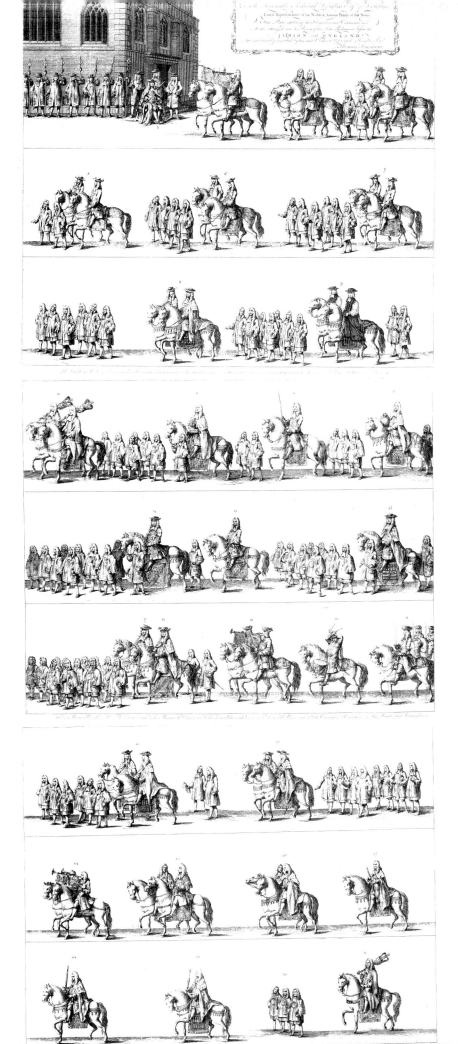

The Riding of Parliament
This depiction probably records the procession of 23 April 1685
Drawn by Roderick Chalmers, later engraved by Alexander Kincaid

Unlike its English counterpart, the Scottish parliament was always a single chamber assembly. The only known depiction of the Scottish parliament in session is an engraving published in Chatelain and de Gueudeville's Atlas Historique, published in 1720, and known as The Downsitting of the Scottish Parliament. By the time the engraving was made, a fourth estate had been added, consisting of commissioners of the shires. The engraving shows the throne occupied by the monarch's representative, the Lord High Commissioner, and on the table in the central area are set the Honours of Scotland.

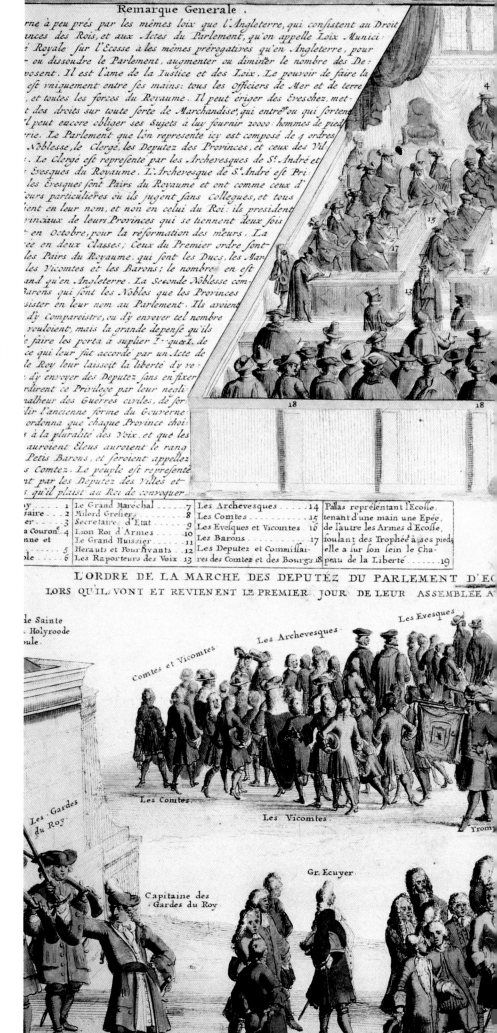

The Downsitting of the Scottish Parliament, 1680s
This fanciful representation of the Scottish parliament meeting in Old Parliament Hall is the earliest known depiction of the sitting of the Scots parliament. From Chatelain's Atlas Historique, 1720

Suite de la Remarque.

ſon Parlement, Les Deputez s'étant rendus à Edimbourg Capitale
à l'Abbaye de St. Croix, ou Holyroode houle, pour proceder à la
le qu'on la repreſente ici: s'étant rendus au Parlement en cette
miſſaire ſe place ſur ſon Throne, et prés de lui les Grands O
et aux deux côſtez les Prelats et les Pairs ſeculiers; Les Depu
droite et ceux des Bourgs à la gauche. Les Ornemens Roy
table par le Grand Connétable et par le Grand Maréchal
par l'Eveſque d'Edimbourg, on fait la Lecture de la Lis
te le Grand Chancelier s'aprochant du Throne ſe met à
mains du Grand Commiſſaire, la Commiſſion du Roi, qu'u
pour en faire la lecture. On lit en ſuite la Formule qu
dre de l'Aſſemblée, aprés quoi Lion Roi d'Armes dé
les Seigneurs et Deputez ſelon leurs rangs. Le Gran
en ſuite les intentions du Roi qui ſont plus ample
Chancelier; on fait prêter ſerment aux Deputez et
ſaires pour dreſſer la reponſe à la lettre du Roi
l'Election des Commiſſaires, appellez Seigneurs
pour dreſſer les Actes qui doivent eſtre pr
pour cela on choiſit 8 Eveſques, 8 Milords, 8
geois pour les 4 ordres du Royaume. Voici
der à cette Election: Les Eveſques choiſiſſe
ſent 1 Duc, 1 Marquis et 6 Comtes. Les S
Ecleſiaſtiques qui ſont ordinairement les
6 Eveſques. Ces 16 Commiſſaires avec
la Couronne qui ſont Commiſſaires dan
ſiſſent les 16 autres, ſavoir 8 pour
les Bourgs. Tous ces préliminaire
conduit le Grand Commiſſaire d
vient les autres jours au Parle
Il y a encore un Parlement j
fut etabli par Iacques V. avan
un mouvant qui alloit par le
et interpreter les Loix. Les É
ques Cours ſouveraines de Gra
matieres criminelős de chaque
officiers Ordinaires, il y a enc
ditaire qui juge les cauſes ci

Parlement

Trompettes

Pourſuivants

Les Commiſſaires des Comtez, et des Bourgs, et des Villes.

ENT.
Lords   Barons

Lords Advocats.

Les Commiſſaires des Comtez, Bourgs

Heraut   d' Ar   mes.

Lyon Roy d' Armes.

Le Grand Huiſſier

Marq: qui porte la co
du Roy

Pourſuivants

1 Maſſier.

Maréchal

Le Grand Commiſſaire
Gr. Connetable

Celui qui   porte la
Commiſſion   du Roy.

Plan of Old Parliament House, showing its conversion into the Courts of Justice
From Maitland's *The History of Edinburgh*

Old Parliament Hall
The most notable feature of the old Scottish Parliament is the great hall, 123 feet long and 42 feet wide, with a magnificent 60 foot high timber roof resting on corbels. The last meeting of the old Scottish parliament took place in this hall on 28 April 1707, opposite

His Majesty's Master of Works, Sir James Murray, was engaged to design the Scottish Parliament and a site was selected. The foundation stone was laid on 3 August 1632 in the upper part of the Kirkyard of St Giles, situated on Edinburgh's ancient spine, the Royal Mile. Parliament House, paid for by the citizens of Edinburgh, was completed several years later at a cost equivalent to £10,555 sterling. The dignified building and its ornamentation, made of stone from a number of local quarries, was characteristic of the mature "court" style of Murray's architecture. Above the Renaissance style doorway stood the royal arms flanked by statues of Justice and Mercy. The building's most notable feature and the one which has remained unaltered to this day is the great hall, 123 feet long and 42 feet wide, with a magnificent 60 feet high timber roof resting on corbels.

Scotland had its own parliament until the Treaty of Union with England. The crowns of England and Scotland had been united since 1603, but when the people of Scotland learnt of the Articles of Union large hostile crowds demonstrated in Parliament Close. Within the House itself the sessions continued unabated and the thirty Commissioners acting for England and a like number for Scotland decided in favour of union on 25 March 1707. By the end of the following month, the supreme legislature of Scotland adjourned to assemble no more. The last meeting of the old Scottish parliament took place on 28 April 1707 and concluded with the Chancellor's famous words: "Now there's ane end of ane auld sang."

The parliament building thus became redundant only 68 years after its completion. Until 1779, Parliament Hall retained much of its furnishings and features from its days as a legislature. The building was significantly altered at the beginning of the nineteenth century when the architect Robert Reid encased the original building with a neo-classical facade (although elements of the original building still remain). Fire destroyed much of Parliament Square in 1824, though Parliament House survived and still stands

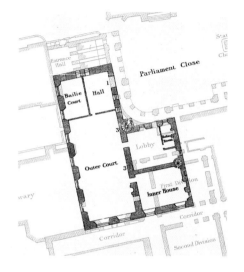

today as home to the Courts of Justice and Advocates Library.

The spirit of Scottish democracy lived on and was aptly described by George Davie in *The Democratic Intellect* (1961),

"... Scotland, which was still national, though no longer nationalist, continued to preserve its European influence as a spiritual force, more than a century after its political identity disappeared."

Old Parliament House, Edinburgh
Engraving of the Old Parliament House showing the royal arms flanked by statues of Justice and Mercy above the Renaissance style doorway

The making of the new Scottish Parliament

Chapter ten

The making of the new Scottish Parliament

When Scotland convened a parliament in Edinburgh in the spring of 1999, the first for almost 300 years, it was on one level the resumption of an ancient institution, and on another the creation of a completely new one. Despite the union of the parliaments, and the earlier coming together of the crowns of England and Scotland when James VI of Scotland became James I of England, as well as a great deal of cross border interaction, both benign and hostile over the preceding centuries, Scotland was still very much a country with its own distinct legal and educational systems, its own banknotes and its own cultural identity. The crowds that came to watch the Queen take her journey along the Royal Mile to open the new parliament's first session in the Church of Scotland's Assembly Hall in Edinburgh were modest in size, and a little bemused in their response. Was this their Queen, the Queen of Scotland, or was it a representative of London?

The mood was not exactly triumphalist, but it was a moment with real national resonance, one with a genuine sense of occasion. Despite themselves, even the most sceptical Scots found themselves glued to their television screens watching an opening ceremony that included not much pomp, but a fair bit of Gaelic singing in the chamber, and poems read by school children. It was an event with complex and contradictory meanings, one that transcended political boundaries, one that those who saw Scotland's future

as an independent nation state could share with those who regarded the new parliament as a means to strengthening Scotland's position within the United Kingdom, and even with those who had opposed the idea of a devolved parliament altogether.

But for all the sense of continuity and the implied rediscovery of national roots, Scotland's parliament created in the wake of the act of devolution passed by the United Kingdom parliament in Westminster is a very different institution from the one that the Act of Union dissolved in 1707. This was, for a start, the first parliament that Scotland had ever elected on the basis of universal suffrage, the first Scottish parliament that women had been allowed to play a part in and the first parliament in Britain which used a proportional voting system. To the late Donald Dewar, Scotland's very first First Minister, the parliament's principal progenitor, it was an emotional, intellectual and cultural challenge, rather than a matter of political expediency. This was not the return of an old institution, it was the beginning of a completely new one.

From the earliest stages of the planning of the new parliament, architecture was an important part of the equation. The question of where the parliament would meet, and what its building would be like, were the subject of as much thought as how the parliament would operate, how many members it would have, how they would be elected, how the parliament would conduct its business and what its powers would be. In fact thinking

about the architectural issues that a parliament building raised was an essential tool that was used to explore the political and procedural questions. Very early on in the process, Donald Dewar, the Secretary of State for Scotland as he then was, set out to create a parliamentary landscape that looked for constructive dialogue between politicians more than confrontation. It was an ambition that would come to be seen symbolically reflected in the shape of a chamber that abandoned the Westminster configuration of opposed sets of benches, in favour of a more unified semi-circular layout. Equally important was the creation of a committee-based executive system that would require meeting rooms for smaller groups of members to concentrate on specific issues forming as important a part of the architectural composition as the main chamber itself.

In September 1997, as the Scots prepared to vote in a referendum on devolution for the second time in a quarter of a century, a team in the Scottish Office led by Chief Architect Dr John Gibbons began to work on the practical issues that would need to be dealt with to build a permanent home for the parliament.

The birth of Scotland's most significant new political institution in three centuries has been far from easy, and was marked by much sadness. Donald Dewar died in office, not long after the death of Enric Miralles, the architect of the Parliament that Dewar chose. Miralles had succumbed to a brain tumour tragically early in his career, with the design of his first major project complete but not yet realised. The parliamentary building now taking shape in Edinburgh is a fitting monument to both of them. It is a powerful and original work of architecture, one that deals with the demands of a complex site, engaging with both Edinburgh's historic urban setting and its dramatic landscape.

Scotland's long abolished ancient parliament had characteristics in common with both its French and English equivalents. Like England in the early days, it had been dependent on the monarch, and had followed the Scottish kings on their perambulations around the country; parliaments met in Stirling as well as Edinburgh. Like the French, it was a single chamber, in which all the estates sat together. It met only occasionally, usually to deal with specific issues of royal policy.

In physical terms the Parliament abolished by the Act of Union of 1707 was, unlike Westminster, not the product of a series of gradual accretions over the centuries, but a relatively new building, one that was constructed especially for the purpose in a single, rapid step. This was a Parliament that was the product of the kind of job-creating impulse that is entirely modern. In the seventeenth century the Stuart court in London made it clear that if Scotland's parliament was going to stay in Edinburgh, with all the economic opportunities it brought in its wake for wig makers, fencing masters, courtesans and inn

keepers, it would need an impressive new building. At the prompting of a Charles I in 1632 "frightened at the lack of convenient and fit roumes within this burgh", Edinburgh's city fathers responded with alacrity, creating a great vaulted hall designed by James Murray with fine hammer-beam roof on a site halfway down the Royal Mile between the Castle and Holyrood. It was a process very close to the construction of a museum or a convention centre with taxpayers' money in the twentieth century. It was the economic spin-offs that were as attractive as the institution itself.

The Parliament was the seat of Scotland's highest Courts of Justice, as well as its legislature and after the Act of Union, the old chamber was used exclusively as the law court that it remains to this day. In 1804 it was given a new face by Robert Reid who put a classical facade on the street front, but behind it the original structure is still intact.

Scotland's recent pursuit of a new definition of its identity has taken a variety of forms. At the end of the 1970s, the former Royal High School, Playfair's version of the Parthenon on Calton Hill, in the city centre, had already been converted for use as a new Parliament when the electorate rejected the whole idea of devolved government. Almost twenty years later, when the Blair government tried again, the new parliament was a clean sheet. Labour went into the Westminster election of 1997 with a commitment

to a second referendum on the question of repatriating a tier of government to Scotland. Once the electorate had backed this move and also endorsed the idea of a parliament with tax-raising powers, the question of the practical realities of accommodating a parliament had to be addressed.

The Scottish Office – the forerunner of the Scottish Executive – had been busy exploring the issues of a home for the new parliament, even before the vote had taken place. Their first finding after considering the potential of the mothballed High School building was that it simply wasn't big enough for the purpose. Where then should it go? Should Scotland's Parliament be in Edinburgh, its capital city, at all? With the history of a peripatetic parliament following the monarch around Scotland, Stirling, where the Scottish kings were traditionally crowned, might have been considered as just as much a historically credible location as Edinburgh. Certainly it would have been closer to the country's geographic centre of gravity. And if the new parliament was looking to establish its roots in Scotland's largest and most populous city, then Glasgow would clearly have been the choice. Indeed, there was considerable lobbying from a range of cities outside Edinburgh, if not for the chamber itself, then at least for a share of any new ministerial offices that might be established. But in the immediate aftermath of the referendum, the Secretary of State announced clearly that the parliament's site would be in Edinburgh.

Feasibility studies

Leith: Benson and Forsyth

Benson and Forsyth looked at the Leith waterfront, on a site adjacent to the Scottish Office building at Victoria Quay, designed by RMJM. Their study went far beyond a diagram to test massing and accommodation, and amounted to a detailed architectural proposal in their distinctive Corbusian style.

Calton Hill: Page and Park Architects

Page and Park examined the possibility of making use of the original St Andrew's House building. The site faced the Royal High School, that had been fitted out as a parliamentary chamber before the first attempt at devolved government failed in the 1970s. Their study suggested a mixture of refurbishment and new building.

Haymarket: RMJM

RMJM looked at two different sites: Holyrood and Haymarket. This one close to Haymarket station, on Edinburgh's western edge, was not pursued.

Holyrood: RMJM

The option for the Holyrood site was the favoured choice for the new Scottish Parliament.

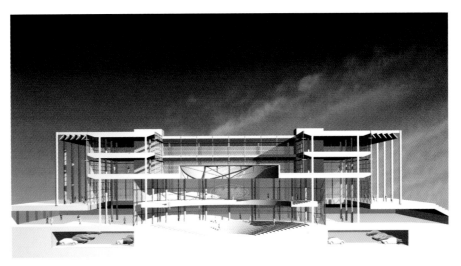

The Scottish Office prepared a list of potential sites in the city, as the first step in a long drawn out process that eventually gave birth to the parliament building that is now taking shape at the foot of Edinburgh's Royal Mile, adjacent to the Palace of Holyroodhouse. The search went on at the same time that the Scottish Office team began exploring exactly what kind of accommodation it was that the new parliament would require. Working in collaboration with Edinburgh City Council, the Scottish Office considered the possibility both of conversions of existing buildings and of sites for new buildings. In all thirty six sites were scrutinised, which produced a shortlist of three: Leith Docks, Haymarket Station, and St Andrew's House, the headquarters of the Scottish Office accommodated in Sir William Kinninmouth's Mussolinesque megalith above Waverley Station. Each site was assigned to an architectural practice, charged with testing its suitability for accommodating the required brief. Benson and Forsyth, architects of the new Museum of Scotland, worked on the Leith site but, in the end,

it was seen as too far from the city centre to be regarded as truly part of Edinburgh. From Glasgow, Page and Park produced an impressive scheme to transform and expand St Andrew's House. But despite its sophistication, if parliament had used St Andrew's House, it would have meant finding alternative accommodation for some 1000 civil servants. The Edinburgh office of RMJM produced a study for the Haymarket site which would certainly have been large enough but in the end was regarded as not being dignified enough for a Parliament. This shortlist was extended to include a fourth site, on land owned by the Scottish and Newcastle brewery, next to the Palace of Holyroodhouse. The Scottish Office team had already considered the site, but initially ruled it out – the owners wanted to hold onto the land past the Parliament's planned opening date. When they changed their minds, and offered to sell immediately, RMJM's studies showed that it was eminently suitable. With its position at the foot of the Royal Mile, close to the Palace of Holyroodhouse, it was both open

enough to allow for a powerful new landmark work of architecture, and still connected with Edinburgh's historic fabric and so charged with symbolic significance as part of Scotland's ancient seat of power.

After a brief consideration of the possibility of a commercial development, or a private finance initiative, or even of a building with commercial sponsors, as the route to achieving the new building, the Scottish Office opted for an architectural competition to find a designer, and to manage the development themselves. Right from the start it was made clear that the competition was to find an architect, rather than a design. Determined to avoid the occasionally unpleasant surprises thrown up by the anonymous open competition system, the Scottish Office opted instead for a process that began with the creation of a long list of twelve architectural firms selected from the seventy who responded to an initial advertisement. All twelve architects were interviewed by a selection panel chaired by the Secretary of State, made up of Joan O'Connor, past president of the Royal Institute of Architecture in

Ireland, Professor Andy MacMillan, the distinguished architect and former head of the Mackintosh School of Architecture, and the broadcaster Kirsty Wark, along with senior management representatives from the Scottish Office. Interviews for the first stage had taken place in the Scottish Office's London headquarters in Dover House and Victoria Quay in Edinburgh. The architects represented an enormous range from Groep Planning of Bruges who had built the Flemish Parliament in Brussels to Allies and Morrison, architects of the British Embassy in Dublin. Those twelve were reduced to five firms who were invited to produce a detailed design: Michael Wilford, from London, Richard Meier and Keppie Design (from New York and Glasgow), Rafael Vinoly with Reiach and Hall (New York), and Denton Corker Marshall with Glass Murray Architects (Glasgow and Melbourne), and Enric Miralles from Barcelona. At this stage the architects' references were taken up, and the selection panel embarked on a series of site visits to look at the selected architects' work for themselves.

Judging panel, left to right
Robert Gordon, Donald Dewar, Kirsty Wark, John Gibbons, Joan O'Connor and Andy MacMillan

The second round of interviews took place in the spring of 1998 in Glasgow's Meridian Court, an office block occupied by the Scottish Office. Competitors were asked to restrict their presentation to six information boards and a model. The idea was to concentrate on their design strategies rather than on the elaboration of their presentation skills. But all of the participants ended up bringing elaborate models with them. Vinoly, designer of the spectacular Tokyo City forum, had his impounded at Glasgow airport. Officials at the Scottish Office were surprised when the customs men came on the line, to say that they had an architect with them who claimed that he was coming to see the Secretary of State, and that they were proposing to charge £4,000 in import duty on his excess baggage.

Of all the participants in the competition, Miralles was perhaps the most adventurous choice. His few built works to date in Spain were powerful but modestly scaled, his critical reputation was high but his office was small. However the poetic intensity of his vision for the Holyrood site, and his sense of energy and intellectual inquiry persuaded the selection panel to make him their unanimous choice. Famously, Miralles' initial submission had as its centre point a photograph that he had taken as a student of a beach on which

an upturned boat had been turned into a turf-roofed hut. Miralles was conveying the image of a building that grew naturally out of its site, stretching away to the lush green meadows of Arthur's Seat, rather than sitting heavily on it, and it hinted at the gently curved shell-like shapes that he planned to build.

Between his first and second interviews, Miralles had opted to create a partnership with the Scottish practice RMJM, so as to provide for an efficient management structure to realise the commission.

In comparison to the other shortlisted designs, Miralles' proposed a much less formal building, one that used organic shapes rather than sharp geometrical forms. The site moves from the mediaeval stone-faced alleys of the Royal Mile at one end to the open spaces of Arthur's Seat. The site is occupied by a huge diversity of buildings, from the battered hulk of the old Queensberry House at one end, to a clutter of more recent structures straggling off toward the south.

Miralles, alone of the competitors, advocated the retention of Queensberry House that stands on part of the site. Built by the mason James Smith, the once grand house has had a chequered history. Begun in 1681 it was completed by 1686 for the Earl of Lauderdale, who promptly sold it to the first Duke of Queensberry. The Act

of Union started its journey in the house, as its signatories hid from the angry mob outside. Its later history took a bizarre turn, and there were lurid tales of orgies and decadence. The house was subsequently made into flats, then sold in 1803 to the board of ordnance for use as a barracks. The interiors were stripped of all their characteristic decoration, and the roof was raised by a storey in 1808. Then it became a refuge for paupers and finally a geriatric hospital which was closed in 1995, by which time there was little trace of its original form. It was acquired by Scottish and Newcastle, whose giant brewery occupied the rest of the site. It was once responsible for brewing one quarter of Scotland's beer, and also the site of their headquarters building. But Scottish and Newcastle finally opted to move operations to an out of town site, and their offices were also relocated.

Miralles' design addresses both the urban imperatives of the site and the specific qualities of the brief. He conceived the project in three major sections: a six-storey building to the west of the site, to accommodate members' offices, a foyer linking the office block by way of a refurbished Queensberry House to the third element, the parliamentary chamber.

Once the parliament itself came into being in its temporary home on Edinburgh's

Mound, Miralles had a new client. He was now working for the parliament itself, rather than for the Scottish Executive, and inevitably many of the assumptions on which his design was based came under close scrutiny again. The major architectural issue that was reopened was the shape of the debating chamber. Miralles designed a curved boomerang structure. Once the parliament's first Presiding Officer, Sir David Steel, was installed, the shape was revisited. Steel went on a fact-finding tour that took in many of the European Parliaments that the Scottish Office team had looked at in the early stages to see for himself what such chambers would be like and modifications were subsequently made to its shape. The question was that of atmosphere in the chamber. Nobody liked the idea of confrontation, but MSPs wanted to create a sense of occasion.

At the same time the scale of the building began to increase to accommodate the demands of the parliamentarians and their officials. There was no one major change, but a lot of small-scale steps that had a major cumulative effect. It was decided that committees for example would need twelve clerks not eight to run them. The press gallery was enlarged. The size of the members' offices went up too, though at 15m² each, they are much more modest than the new Portcullis House at Westminster which allows 25m². In the end, all this served to nearly double the size of the complex from 17 000 m² to 32 000m², with predictable impacts on the cost of the building.

As part of the preparations an archaeological investigation of Queensberry House was undertaken, which revealed the structure to be in even worse condition than was expected. It was never Miralles' intention to restore the long-lost interiors to their period condition, but the shell of the house would be given more or less its original form. But the costs of the exercise rose as the structure was revealed to be in extremely poor condition and as successive layers of later additions were peeled away.

Miralles continued to refine his design. His own sketch books record a continually evolving sequence of drawings made in pencil that formed the starting point for the technical drawings. In his Barcelona studio, Miralles, his wife and partner Benedetta Tagliabue and chief lieutenant Joan Callis provided a forum for him to discuss and refine his ideas, while teams of model makers worked with cardboard on a series of working models that were a vital design tool. In Edinburgh at the offices of RMJM a second team was set up to work on the execution of the building.

With parliament committing itself to Miralles' design, work went ahead on letting contracts, but the project then found itself the subject of a hot debate about cost. Initial estimates had focused only on building costs, without factoring in professional fees, fixtures and fittings and VAT. The increase in size of course only made the apparent increase in cost more pronounced. But by the time of Miralles' untimely death, the design and the cost plan had been finalised and agreed at a total cost of £195 million. Miralles had also made up his mind about the physical character of the building and its finishes. In material terms the intention was to reflect the character of Scotland as a whole, rather than a specifically Edinburgh tradition. To Miralles that meant granite rather than sandstone. But the building is not a stone monolith. Miralles creates a pattern of shapes and fills them at random with slate, granite, oak and varieties of steel, going from a matt lead-like effect to shiny stainless steel.

With construction underway, the superstructure of the MSP building was topped out at the beginning of 2001. The new Parliament itself, a potent landmark for a shifting political landscape, as well as a signpost for a lost talent that would have helped to define a new architectural generation will be opened before Scotland goes to the polls for the second time.

Denton Corker Marshall competition scheme

The Australian practice, Denton Corker
Marshall, first came into prominence
with a well regarded, but unbuilt design
for the Australian Parliament in Canberra.
Their proposal for Edinburgh submitted
with Glass Murray used the landscape
of Arthur's Seat as the starting point for
a boldly modelled design planned around
a sophisticated sequence of public spaces.

Richard Meier competition scheme

The New York based architect Richard Meier is best known for the new Getty Museum in Los Angeles. His submission with Keppie Design reflects his charasteristic design vocabulary of white walls and pure geometry that is based on a reworking of Le Corbusier's themes.

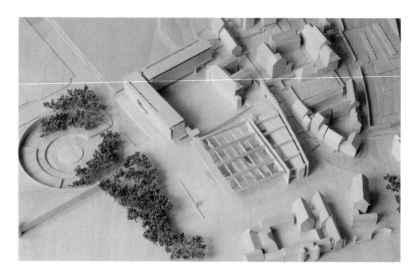

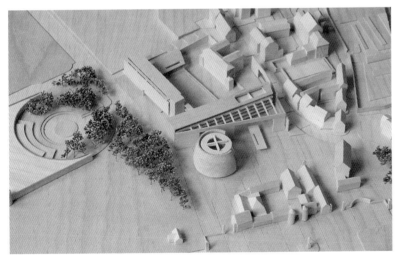

Raphael Vinoly competition scheme

Working with Edinburgh-based practice
Reiach and Hall, Raphael Vinoly, architect
of the recently completed Tokyo civic forum,
proposed a glass-walled circular debating
chamber, topped by a dramatic floating disc.

Michael Wilford and Partners competition scheme

Michael Wilford, responsible for the new British Embassy in Berlin, and for the Lowry Centre, Salford, proposed a Parliament that would allow the public to use its roof as an outdoor civic forum, marked by a prominent stone tower, with proceedings relayed on a giant screen.

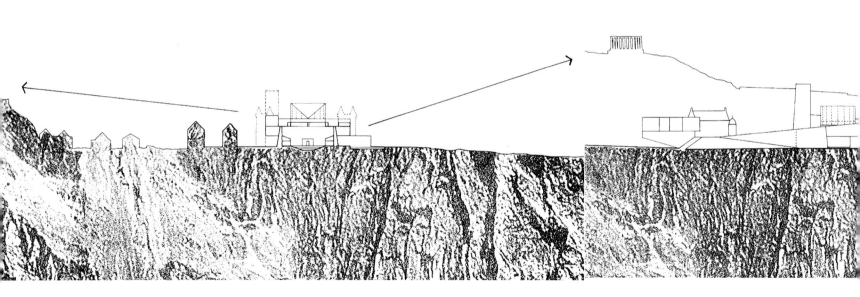

EMBT/RMJM winning competition scheme

The competition was won by Enric Miralles
from Barcelona, in collaboration with
the Edinburgh office of RMJM.

Enric Miralles' initial submission
for the parliament competition suggested
an architectural approach, more than
it defined a design. He proposed a building
that was of its site, rather than imposed,
as a monument, on it. The imagery of
upturned fishing boat hulls that enlivened
his drawings offered a glimpse of an organic
architectural form, scattered in discrete
fragments across the site rather than
dominating it. Developing the project Enric
Miralles and Benedetta Tagliabue, working
with the Edinburgh architects RMJM, have
turned these poetic intentions into a solid
form, one that accomodates and defers to
its historic neighbours, and its remarkable
natural setting, without losing its own sense
of importance.

EMBT /RMJM competition submission

Enric Miralles wrote: "The parliament should belong to a broader thought. The specific place should not be crucial. The parliament building should come out of a clear and strong statement ... in a way independent of site circumstances ... Any strong statement should carry political implications ... The parliament is a form in people's mind. We have the feeling that the building should be land ... built out of land ... To carve in the land the form of gathering of people together not a building in a park nor a garden ..."

EMBT /RMJM competition submission

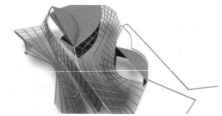

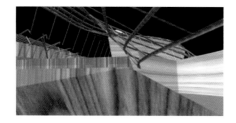

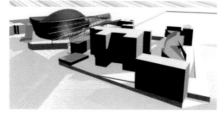

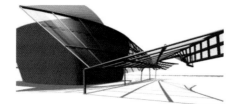

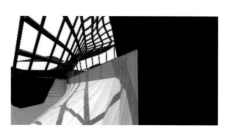

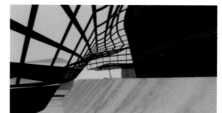

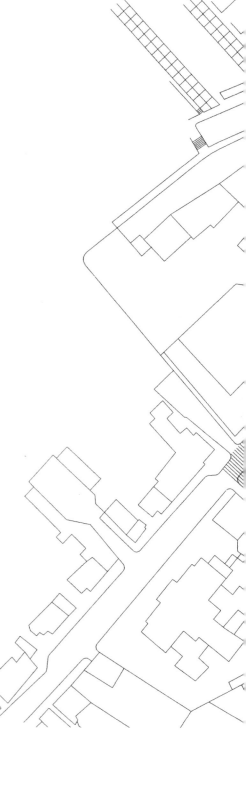

CLAITH CROSS

Canongate and Horse Wynd elevations

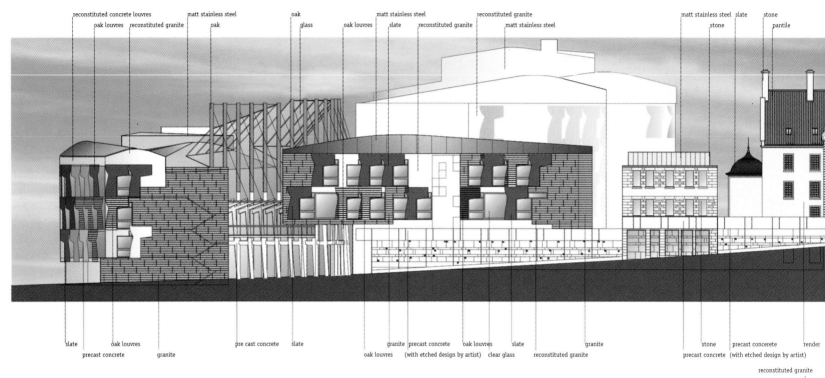

reconstituted concrete louvres
oak louvres   reconstituted granite
matt stainless steel
oak
oak
glass
oak louvres
matt stainless steel
slate
reconstituted granite
reconstituted granite
matt stainless steel
matt stainless steel   slate
stone
stone
stone
pantile

slate
precast concrete
oak louvres
granite
pre cast concrete
slate
oak louvres
granite
precast concrete
(with etched design by artist)
oak louvres
clear glass
slate
reconstituted granite
granite
stone
precast concrete
precast concerete
(with etched design by artist)
render

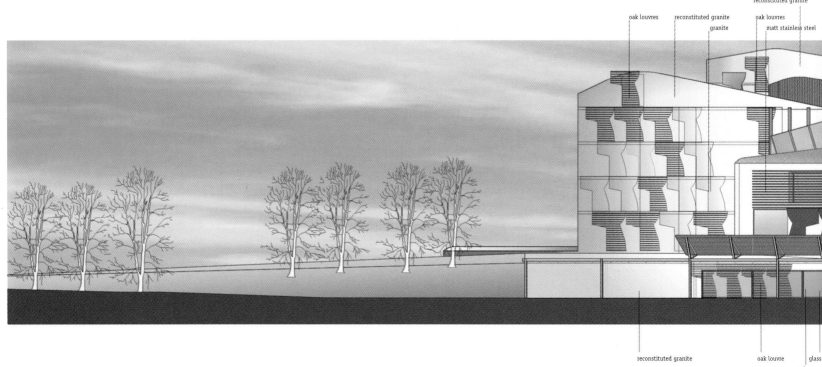

oak louvres   reconstituted granite
granite
oak louvres
reconstituted granite
matt stainless steel

reconstituted granite
oak louvre
glass
oak

stone   lead   stone   granite   slate

matt stainless steel   oak louvres

render

precast concrete

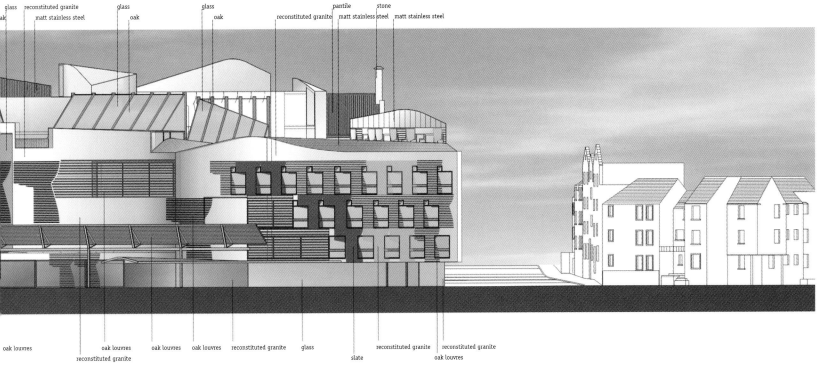

glass   reconstituted granite   glass   glass   pantile   stone

oak   matt stainless steel   oak   oak   reconstituted granite   matt stainless steel   matt stainless steel

oak louvres   oak louvres   oak louvres   oak louvres   reconstituted granite   glass   reconstituted granite   reconstituted granite

reconstituted granite   slate   oak louvres

Landscape plan

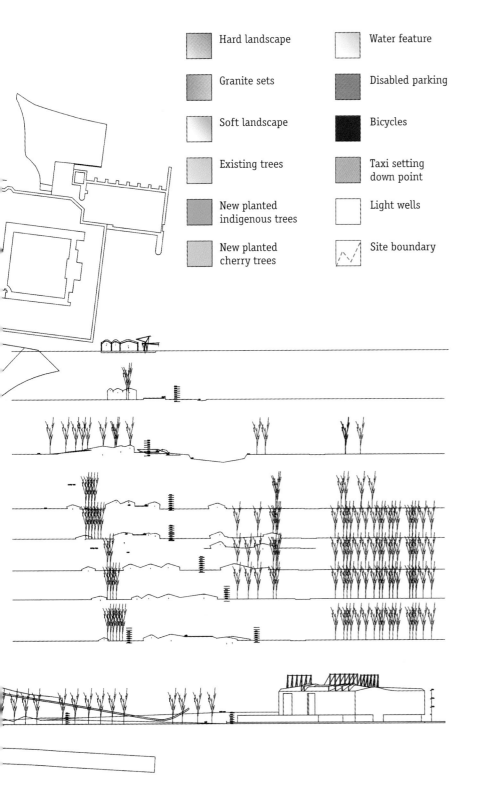

	Hard landscape		Water feature
	Granite sets		Disabled parking
	Soft landscape		Bicycles
	Existing trees		Taxi setting down point
	New planted indigenous trees		Light wells
	New planted cherry trees		Site boundary

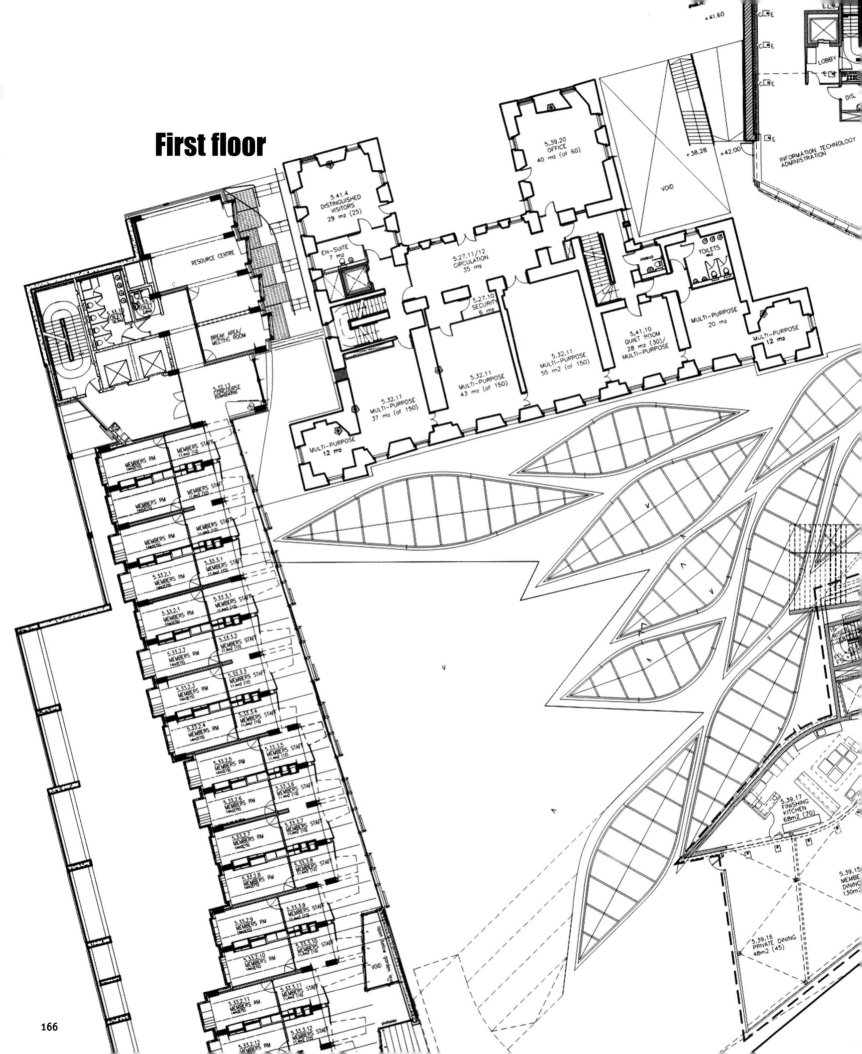

First floor

5.41.4
DISTINGUISHED
VISITORS
29 m2 (25)

5.39.20
OFFICE
40 m2 (of 60)

VOID

+38.28   +42.00

INFORMATION TECHNOLOGY
ADMINISTRATION

LOBBY

RESOURCE CENTRE

EN-SUITE
7 m2

5.27.11/12
CIRCULATION
35 m2

TOILETS

MULTI-PURPOSE
20 m2

BREAK AREA/
MEETING ROOM

5.27.10
SECURITY
6 m2

5.41.10
QUIET ROOM
28 m2 (30)/
MULTI-PURPOSE

MULTI-PURPOSE
12 m2

CONCOURSE

5.32.11
MULTI-PURPOSE
43 m2 (of 150)

5.32.11
MULTI-PURPOSE
55 m2 (of 150)

5.32.11
MULTI-PURPOSE
37 m2 (of 150)

MULTI-PURPOSE
12 m2

MEMBERS RM

MEMBERS STAFF

MEMBERS RM

MEMBERS STAFF

MEMBERS RM

MEMBERS STAFF

5.33.2.1
MEMBERS RM

5.33.3.1
MEMBERS STAFF

5.33.2.1
MEMBERS RM

5.33.3.1
MEMBERS STAFF

5.33.2.2
MEMBERS RM

5.33.3.2
MEMBERS STAFF

5.33.2.3
MEMBERS RM

5.33.3.3
MEMBERS STAFF

5.33.2.4
MEMBERS RM

5.33.3.4
MEMBERS STAFF

5.33.2.5
MEMBERS RM

5.33.3.5
MEMBERS STAFF

5.33.2.6
MEMBERS RM

5.33.3.6
MEMBERS STAFF

5.33.2.7
MEMBERS RM

5.33.3.7
MEMBERS STAFF

5.33.2.8
MEMBERS RM

5.33.3.8
MEMBERS STAFF

5.33.2.9
MEMBERS RM

5.33.3.9
MEMBERS STAFF

5.33.2.10
MEMBERS RM

5.33.3.10
MEMBERS STAFF

VOID

5.33.2.11
MEMBERS RM

5.33.3.11
MEMBERS STAFF

5.33.2.12
MEMBERS RM

5.33.3.12
MEMBERS STAFF

5.39.17
FINISHING
KITCHEN
68m2 (70)

5.39.15
MEMBERS
DINING
130m2

5.39.16
PRIVATE DINING
48m2 (45)

+42.00

+38.28

LMR

5.39.27
TEA POINT
5.8M2

LOBBY
8.2 sqm

TOILET

ITSD ROOM
16.4M2

5.36.4
BROADCASTING AND
RELATION STAFF
56.7m2

TOILET

5.29.2
PRESS CONFER
< 120.60m2

LOBBY
+43.30

+43.30 +41.650

+42.60

BOOTHS

+43.70

+42.60

+43.70

5.37.4
HEAD OF
CHAMBER
OFFICE
18m2 (20)

5.37.6
ANTE
ROOM
18m2(15)

P.O. D.P.O.
RETIRAL ROOM
19m2 (25)

MALE
TOILET

L.9

5.37.9
PHOTO / STORAGE
20m2 (20)

5.37.8
MESSENGERS
15m2 (15)

5.37.10
ANNUNCIATOR
15m2 (15)

5.37.7
JOURNAL, TABLE
AND PUBLIC
BILL OFFICE
35m2 (40)

5.37.5
CLERKS (5 NO.)
75m2 (75)

EXTENT OF
TOWERS TENDER

+42.00

5.32.13
CONCOURSE
167m2 (200)

+42.00

5.32.5
LOUNGE
60m2 (60)

+59.075

VOID

5.39.21
BAR
150m2 (150)

FLUES 400⌀

5.32.9
COMMITTEE
ANTE ROOM
15m2 (15)

+42.00

MSP AREA

+43.165

TOILET
8m2

PUBLIC AREA

FFL +42.
FSL +42.

5.32.7
SMALL COMMITTEE ROOM
113m2 (100)

5.32.9
COMMITTEE ANTE
ROOM
15m2

VOID

UP

16
RISER
168.7
270m

2x850 HP

FFL +42.00
FSL +41.90

5.32.7 COMMITTEE ROOM

Assembly chamber

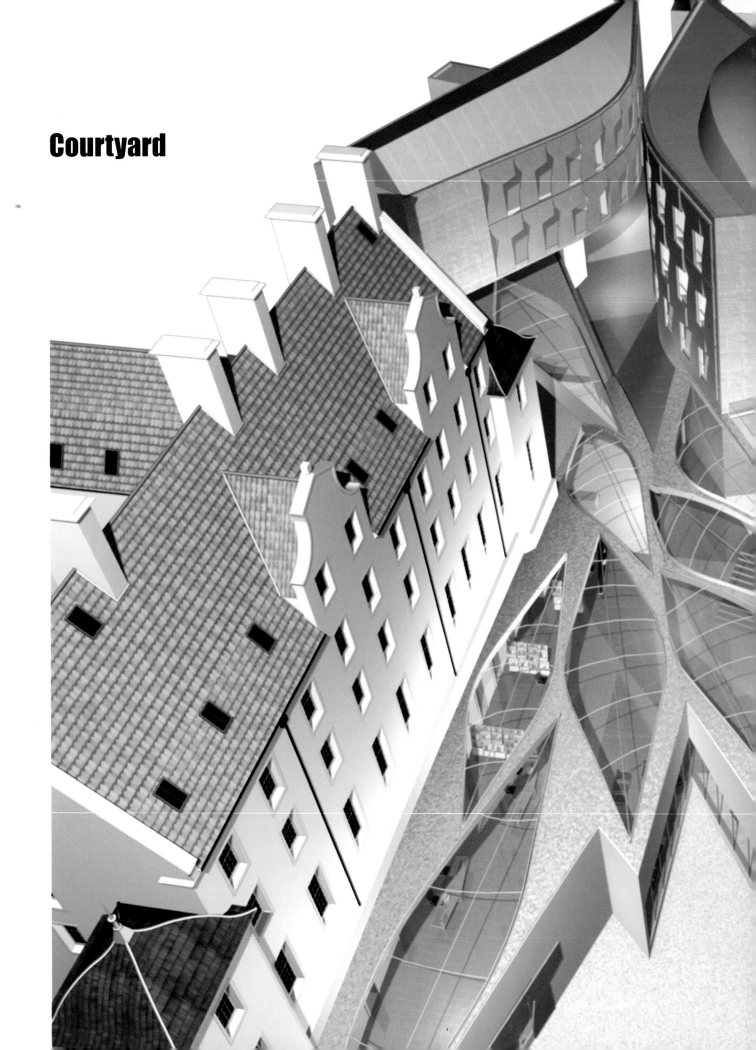

Courtyard

Lobby Areas

Members' offices

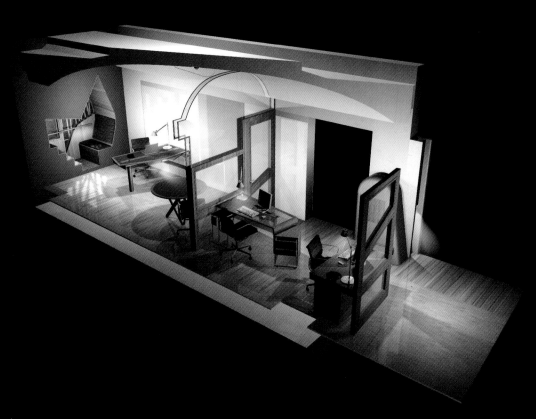

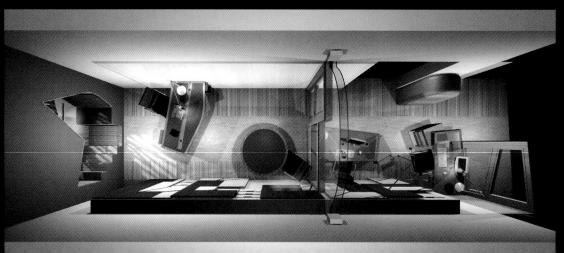

The new Scottish Parliament

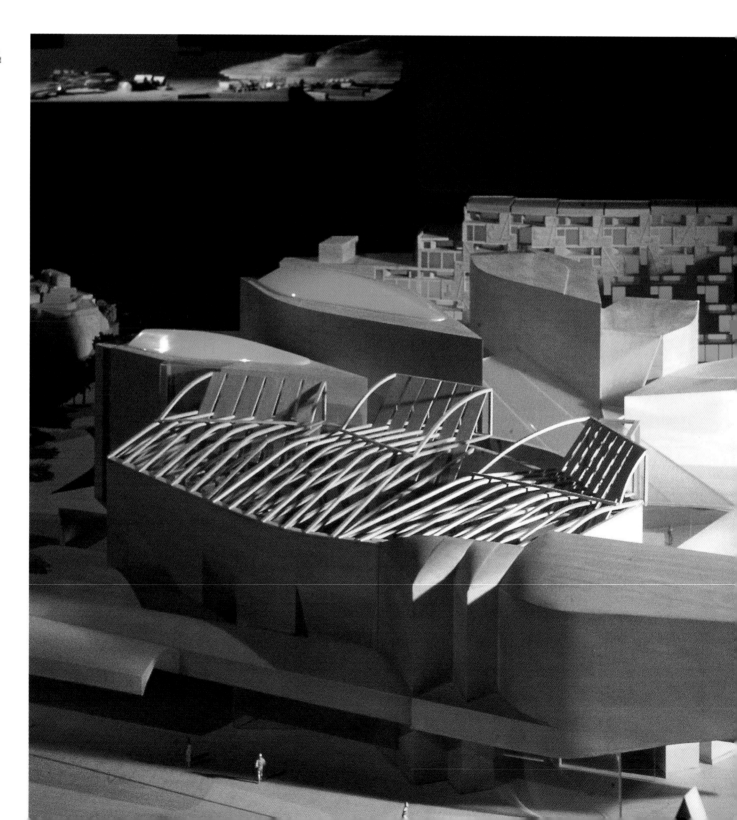

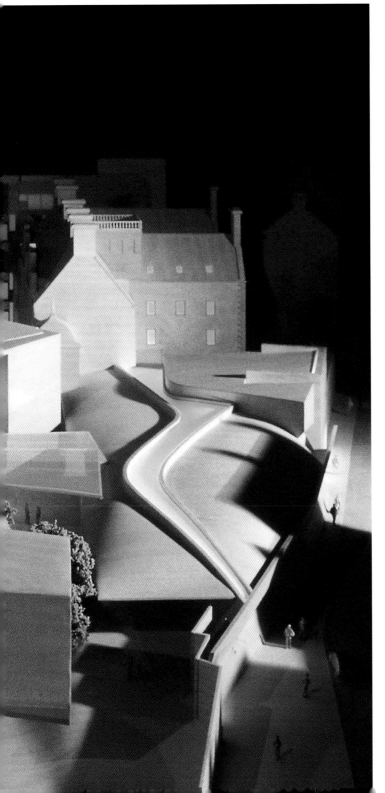

Construction photographs
The superstructure of the MSP building was topped out in 2001

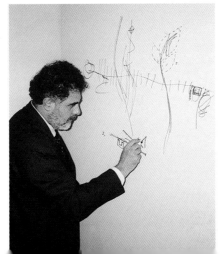

Enric Miralles
Drawing the scheme at the opening of The Architecture of Democracy exhibition, Glasgow 1999

Index

Credits